CW00520634

Table of Content

WELCOME 2

KNOW YOUR WHY 4

FROM PRODUCTS 17

TO SERVICES 17

    INFORMATION PRODUCTS 21

    LEARNING AND DEVELOPMENT 42

OUTSOURCING 58

PRODUCTIVITY AND 67

TIMEKEEPING 67

WHAT MAKES A 79

SUCCESSFUL 79

ENTREPRENEUR 79

BUSINESS MODELS 90

    ADVERTISING MODEL 94

    AFFILIATE MARKETING 97

    E-COMMERCE 101

    COURSES AND COACHING 107

    DIVERSIFY INCOME STREAMS 114

    FREELANCING 115

SELLING BUSINESS 121

FREEDOM NAVIGATOR 128

CHAPTER 1

WELCOME

Welcome to the Freedom Navigator. I've written this book because after five years of being in business myself and running online businesses, I've seen a lot of different models and I've learned a lot of the different ways that lead to success. I have also made mistakes and learned a lot of lessons along the way. What I now know to be true is that anyone can find their own path to financial freedom, but it won't be the same path for everyone. This book is for anyone who is seeking financial freedom and the path less travelled. Read on to discover the path to fulfil your dreams and live the life you desire.

As I started raising my young family, priorities were changing. I realized that what I really wanted was more freedom. I resented all that wasted time and office politics. I was partially motivated by the financial side, to generate a level of income that would allow me the quality of life I wanted to live. But I also wanted to have other sorts of freedom, such as location independence. I wanted a business I could run from home. I wanted a business that didn't require full-time work. I thought it must be possible to start something that lets me generate enough income to live really well, but live life on my terms.

When I started out in business myself, I'd worked in the typical 9 to 5 government job. I'd worked for a university in a tech transfer office for nine years and had come through a corporate model, where I completed an MBA and became a general manager. I was running a team and writing reports for the board while raising investment for projects and reporting back on that investment. I saw in the corporate world, that there is just a lot of money being spent on projects and deployed very inefficiently. We spent our days in meetings, sitting in an office and commuting to and from that office.

In this book, I want to share with you the ways that you can explore this world of online business and find the track that's right for you. Based on your skills and personality, there will be different businesses out there that will suit you and be an easier path. A path of less resistance and a path to financial freedom. I want to help you find the right path in the most efficient way, by giving you an overview and broad understanding of all of the different kinds of online businesses out there. Then you can pick the right one for you.

CHAPTER 2

KNOW YOUR WHY

When you start your business, there's definitely going to be some challenging times ahead. Anybody who says that businesses are easy are lying to you because it's an absolute given that there's going to be challenges. There's going to be extra workload, there's going to be customer, staff or a freelancer issues, financial pressure, and the juggling. Even if everything goes perfectly, you're going to have a juggling act of what you were previously doing in your life alongside your new successful business.

What's absolutely certain is that there's going to be times where it feels hard and that's why being really clear on why you're doing this is extremely important. And the people that I see be really successful in business have spent some time working out why they want to do this extra thing and generate some extra income.

And when they've thought about the reason why, they can then figure out what they need to do and how they need to do it to get the result that they want. In my case, it was very simple. I was working part time hours for an employer. Working for the New Zealand government and three days a week and I was paying a nanny. I was commuting and came home at the end of each week absolutely shattered. One day the nanny sent a photo of her down at the beach with my daughter in the sunshine playing by the sea, while I was stuck in my cubicle plodding away through some spreadsheets. At that point I knew I needed to do something different!

I wasn't sure what I was going to do or how I was going to do it, but I knew there and then I was going to find a way to generate something from home that would let me be at home with my children in those really special years. I didn't want to be missing out on their special moments and outsourcing childcare. That wasn't why I had started a family.

It was really important for me to make sure that whatever business I started gave me freedom. There was no point starting some kind of consulting job that meant I had to travel or be on the phone or be in somebody else's office all the time. I had to be able to do it from home. But my financial targets weren't huge. It happened that I ended up with a very big Amazon business very quickly, but I definitely didn't set out to build an empire.

I wanted something really lean and profitable, something really low time commitment based. So I researched a whole bunch of different business models to find something that I could run in very part time hours from home and generate maybe $5,000 profit a month. And so that seemed very modest when I saw what other people were selling on Amazon and how much money they were making a month. And that's all I set out to do.

When I was choosing my first product, I didn't spend a year waiting to find the perfect product. I just did lots of assessing of lots of different products. I spent more time getting some criteria really clear on what would a good product look like for me based on budget, risk profile and things I was interested in. So that was a much better investment in time than just sitting on Alibaba or Googling product ideas for weeks and months, like I saw a lot of other people doing. I moved quickly into what I wanted to do. I turned ideas over until one clicked into place and felt good enough. Not perfect, but low risk and low budget to get in the game and start learning.

I'd heard about Amazon and then got my first paycheck from Amazon less than seven weeks later. I just got started and threw myself at it. The sooner this new business was up and profitable, the sooner I could quit the day job. It ended up being about nine months before I quit the day job and that was just fine. I see lots of people learn about Amazon and they're still looking for the "perfect product" 9 months in.

By having that extra nine months or so of still earning my day job salary, it meant that I could just take the pressure off myself to get a salary out of my business. I could just focus on growing the business. I was very determined. One of my principles was not to get into debt over this business. We had two family cars, so when I was hoping to be able to stay at home, I sold my car to fund the Amazon project and I was committed. It was like a scorched earth policy, burning the bridges and I sold my car that I used to commute in and used that to pay for the first Amazon course that I did plus the products that I first launched.

I didn't go into any debt at any stage in any of my businesses. And that's still something I've really stuck with all the way through because I see when people are in up to their eyeballs, the interest starting to mount up, the pressure is on, they're worried about making repayments and they've cut off other income streams.

It gets very stressful some days, especially if I've had a bad sleep, not enough exercise or sick kids at home. The little challenges seem much bigger. There's just too much pressure there and I don't ever want to put myself in that situation. I always wanted a business, that if it all goes horribly wrong, it's back to zero. Rather than having bet the house on it and end up mortgaging the house or in serious debt that's gathering interest and getting into a big financial hole. I'm very determined to make this fun as well as a profitable venture.

I was very clear. I wanted to set a role model for my daughter and my son. They were a baby and a toddler at the time I started and are now five and seven. I did not want to run some tacky business. I wanted to run something where I sold quality products. I didn't want to be somebody who bought all the blueprints of how to hack Amazon reviews or the sort of silly clickbait things that you see that sound too good to be true. I'm not a hack using this simple piece of software to find the perfect Amazon product.

All of that stuff that sounds too good to be true is always too good to be true. I decided I would aim, from the very beginning, be a leader in the Amazon world and not just follow other people's programs or other people's strategies. I would actually think of my own way of winning on this platform. It's a big enough platform, there's plenty of room to do things in lots of different ways. Just because one course said to do things one way that that was the only way.

I chose some handmade products. They weren't from China, completely broke all the rules that all the other Amazon courses said to follow. That really worked for me because I ended up in a little quiet patch of my own with no competition, and when everybody else in Amazon ended up in these wars over reviews or price wars or suppliers undercutting them, that never happened to me. I was getting invited to my suppliers' weddings while other people were being ripped off by their suppliers.

I had a really wonderful time by deciding to be innovative and come up with unique products that I would buy myself rather than just copying existing bestsellers that appeal to the mass market of Amazon. It really worked for me to keep my brain in gear and think through strategies that would work rather than just endlessly buy and copy other people's formulas for success. I had some amazing trips to China, Sri Lanka, India and Tibet as soon as I quit the day job, hunting down more products to sell online and meeting my suppliers.

Now for things like Facebook ads where there is one way that this works at the moment, then it's not an area I would try and be innovative, I would just do what works. But with Amazon, it was a wide open platform, so many millions of different products for sale. I could see when the courses that I was doing demonstrated a product as a kind of a case study, loads of people would go and launch that same product. It seemed like madness. And so these people were just sort of copying what was in front of their noses without any original thoughts.

I really wanted to use my Amazon business to establish my-self as a successful entrepreneur. It wasn't just about getting some quick cash, it was about being a successful business owner that would last through that oncoming competition and would be profitable. I saw a lot of people chest beating and posting screenshots of their sales. But then as I started coach-ing and some of these really big sellers started approaching me saying, "Well, my revenue might've been $6 million, but actually I'm running at a loss," it suddenly looked a lot less impressive.

I was always very focused on profit because that was my ticket to freedom. Having a business that made a profit, not just a business with turnover. It had to be part time hours so I could look after the children at home and live in the South Island of New Zealand, rather than have to stay in the capital city and work for the government. Another thing that was re-ally important for me was the opportunity to learn and become good at business.

I saw it as an opportunity to learn a lot of new stuff around business. Amazon was the platform I started on, but that wasn't the end point. It was just one step along the way. Then some of the other information products that have come later, like coaching and courses have been just as much fun and possibly even more lucrative at times given the margins on information products versus the margins on physical products.

Everybody will have a slightly different track through this. Not everybody enjoys Amazon because you've got to spend money before you make money. You've got to buy those prod-ucts up front and be quite creative working with designers and packaging people to create your own private labels. There's a formula, there's a way to do it, the way I teach. Some people just start on Amazon and they just find it a bit daunting. Something else like freelancing suits them a lot better. They'd rather just know they're going to work 20 hours a week and they're going to get paid X dollars an hour, it let's them work from home. And then they've got a couple of days at home to do their own thing or with their family or following their passion or their sports or working for charity or a cause they believe in.

It doesn't matter what your reason is. You might want to build an empire, you might just want to replace your part-time salary and anything in between is absolutely fine. But the most important thing is to know why you're doing it. I see the people that are just trying to make a quick dollar, are not nearly as successful an approach as being really motivated towards the future state that's very clear and very positively framed. And it's been really interesting as an Amazon coach and a business coach seeing lots of people come through the same program with the same access to identical information on an online course. Some people really jump at it, they can't wait to get on to the next module. They do the work after each step and they're really clear on what the result is that they want and they find the motivation a lot easier.

They're working towards something, whereas if someone's just miserable in their day job and looking for a way out, they're moving away from that job, but they haven't got a clear thing that they're working towards. And so those people tend to find it a lot harder. They're sort of operating out of fear and negative feelings rather than being really inspired and moving towards something positive.

The clearer you can get on your reason why and what your future state will look like is important. A great exercise is to stop and just write freehand for a few minutes what your life would look like 12 months from now if you've had a successful business that you've started. Make up the number that you want to earn, your target monthly income. You can say what would have changed in your life. Would you have quit your day job, will you be traveling? Will you be living somewhere else? Will you be working from home? Will you have your own clients? Will you have your own brand? Will you have an online course that you run? Will you be a coach, a successful business coach or a life coach or an agency owner? Will you be running other people's ads or creating content for them?

You might not know exactly what business you run yet. You won't know the mechanics of it, but you might know what kind of future you want and the clearer you are about what your lifestyle looks like, the easier it'll be to build that business to fit your needs, to meet your needs. Then the work will just flow. It's so much easier when you know what you want, than if you just start and bumble along, hoping to follow your nose through a course and pop out on the other hand with the perfect business.

There's always going to be challenges. There's always going to be days where it's easier to watch Netflix, than to write copy for your website, get back onto Google and look for suppliers for a product, start writing Facebook ads or crunching numbers on a different business ideas. I've turned down a lot of social engagements. It's always hard to work before you get the rewards. If you ever need a little flash of inspiration, a couple of good books, you could read: Drive by Steven Pinker, which is very good, all about being really clear about what motivates us.

A great TED Talk by Simon Sinek called Know Your Why. This is a talk that is extremely popular because it transcends different businesses and people. Everybody gets out of bed for a reason. Often we're really busy and working hard without a clear reason why. Why are we doing it and what we want from life. If we get the result that we're working towards, what will that mean to us and why do we want that?

It could be around family, it could be around fame and fortune, it could be a financial target. But even money in the bank doesn't make you happy. It's what you can do because you've got money in the bank. So I've got a horse, I go skiing, I've got children who I pick up from school every afternoon. I get help with the children and all those luxuries are what I enjoy because I've got a successful business. If I was working nine to five in my old day job, I would get a steady paycheck, but I wouldn't get all those other things that I can have because I've got my own business that lets me work part time hours. So it's not just the money that comes in, it's the time I've got free. I can schedule my own weeks, I can decide which days I want to work and when I don't.

That freedom is such a luxury and I never, ever, take it for granted. Every day I've got time with my children, I see other families where the nanny's doing the school run or the children are going to some after school program. I know how lucky I am to have those afternoons with my children from three o'clock and I really, really love it.

Everybody's motivation is different. Some people might be caring for elderly family or working with a charity or cause. Maybe train and get really fit into some sporting events that you would never be able to train for or dedicate the time and energy to with your current commitments. Maybe it's that feeling of scratching your entrepreneurial itch, you've always wanted to start your own business. Or maybe you want to hit $1 million because that's your measure of a successful business, but it's never just the dollars. It's not the numbers. It's what the numbers let you do by being a successful business owner that makes the difference.

Remember it's got to be profitable, not just turnover. Don't let those revenue figures get you too excited. Anyone can make $1 million if they spend $2 million! So you've really got to focus on what comes out of the bottom, what dollars are leftover, not just which ones can come in the top, but which ones are left for you at the end of the day after tax.

I really enjoy working with people one on one about their reasons why they're doing this. I really love understanding what makes people tick. Everybody's motivations and background stories, the role models in their lives that have inspired them are so different. Some people are way more aggressive than me. They want to build huge empires. They measure their success by their headcount or their job title. They want to be the CEO, they want the fancy cars and all of that stuff. And that does nothing for me at all. I drive a battered old car that's full of horse hair and mud and I never take the key out of the ignition. I love rural life in a very relaxed small town and I don't really go for materialistic stuff at all.

Having a horse for me is a huge luxury. It's a very expensive hobby where I live in the mountains where there's no grass. So that's my splurge and what I do for fun, I grew up loving horses. Then I've got the time with the children, and I have built and designed the lifestyle I want.

Some lifestyle design will help you pick the business model that will work best for you. There's no point in creating another 60 or 70 hour a week job to hit some financial target. By then you're going to be absolutely exhausted and worse off than you were when you started. Make sure you design your lifestyle and then make your business fit with that. And there's plenty of business models we're going to share in the coming chapters that will give you lots of ideas and inspiration for different ways that you can hit the lifestyle and business targets in your life. I love seeing how people think, get motivated and inspired.

The other thing you can do as well as professional development is personal development work. There's lots and lots of tips in this book on professional development around podcasts, conferences, courses and coaching and all the things you can do to upscale. Working on yourself is really essential - you are the most important asset in your business. You'll have all sorts of limiting beliefs that you may not be aware of that will cap your level of motivation or ambition. By working on yourself, you might find you set your targets and sights a little higher or you're a bit clearer on why you want them.

There's some really good resources that I'll add some links to as well that you can check out. Tony Robbins is always a really good person to follow and study as a leader of success. His own system is about being the best version of yourself. If you're struggling to get motivated or struggling to find clarity on what you want, then read 'Unleash the Giant Within'. Some of Tony Robbins' other books and live events are really good for helping unlock some of those things that might be circling around in your brain, it's hard to get them clear when you're playing a smaller game. You're much more capable of being way more successful, on a completely different level and completely different terms to what you're currently thinking.

Don't do this bit lightly. Really think and imagine vividly 12 months from now what your life could be like if you had the perfect business, something that was supporting you for the exact lifestyle you wanted. Write down what that lifestyle is, not the details of the business, but how would you live? What would you do every day? When everyone else gets up on a Monday morning and heads off to work in their car What do you wake up and do on a Monday morning? Do you have a coffee in the sun? Hang out in the garden a bit? Go and ride your horse? Go for a run? Yoga? Do you go and hang out with friends and do something social? Are you traveling? Are you even at home? Where would you be? What would you be doing with the typical day when you've got this business that gives you the lifestyle that you dream of?

Then once that's clear, filling in the gaps is easy. There's ways to get there. You just need to know where you want to be and then we can help you get there. So do that exercise now. Just spend five minutes just writing freehand. Just pen and paper. 12 months from now, where would you like to be? How would your life look? What's different by having a successful online business?

CHAPTER 3

FROM PRODUCTS TO SERVICES

The way I got started was actually selling physical products on Amazon. I went through an online course, which was a very interesting experience. It was the first investment I'd made in myself like that. It was about $5,000 U.S. dollars, and over eight modules, I learned the basics through some video sessions on how to set up and run an Amazon business. Of course, being a little bit maverick in my approach to most things, I ignored most of the rules about what kind of products to choose and which country to source from. I went about my Amazon product strategy very differently.

I signed up for that Amazon course and I spent $5,000. However, I could see that some of the people promoting that Amazon course were on a 50% commission as an affiliate, which I'll talk about later. Some of those guys were making $10 million in a day when that product launched for the Amazon course. I spent $5,000 to learn a new set of skills, and somebody who wasn't even selling Amazon products, but just selling the program to their database, were making $10 million in a day. That was interesting.

There was a guy in the program called Rapid Crush with Jason Fladlien. They'd put a lot of great content out through YouTube videos. He did great webinars and had a huge database. Then, the Amazing Selling Machine, which was the course I completed, had some video sales letters. That's a series of short videos in over four sessions, one a week. You'd learn a little bit more about the program, and it would get you hooked.

Then, by the time this video sales series had finished, I was convinced I was about to sign up and do it. I also learned a lot about how the marketing of this information product worked to sell me a course, that I was using to learn about how to become an Amazon seller. I parked all of that. I watched and learned all about Amazon, saw what these other people were doing. I saw the amount of money that the people who developed The Amazing Selling Machine course made, and I saw how much money the affiliates were making. I then went off and started my own first physical products business, and fortunately that went really well. In my first year, I sold over 1.6 million dollars US of a product that I sourced online and was selling for a nice profit margin.

The profit margins wasn't as good as some of those information product courses, or being an affiliate marketer promoting somebody else's course. I saw some people making some outrageous amounts of money doing that. They didn't have to run an ongoing business. They got a big lump sum of commission as the course launched and their audience bought the courses.

Now, there's other courses out there that don't do a big launch once or twice a year, but they have non-stop Facebook ads running. All the time people are seeing those Facebook ads, they go into a database, get some emails, they might watch some videos as part of those emails. They might be invited to watch a webinar and over the next little period of time. Those prospects, the people who are interested in learning about something new, start to like, know and trust the person selling the program. They start to believe in what's possible if they learn those skills and by the time they've gone through the videos, the emails, the webinars, they're ready to purchase that information product themselves.

Sometimes it's a book, sometimes it's a webinar, sometimes there's videos. The format can differ, but really at the essence of it, what is generating a huge amount of profit for those people that create and promote those information products is such a neat model. They create the content once and then they can promote it. It's the investment in the marketing and partnerships to affiliates and splitting the commission. There's some huge wealth to be generated by selling information products.

So after a couple of years on Amazon, I sold my first Amazon business for over a million dollars. I had a good look around at all the other business models out there. I looked at Shopify websites, because e-Commerce was an obvious next progression step from selling products on the Amazon platform, but there were pros and cons with Shopify. So I decided to stick with what I knew and what was working. I started another Amazon brand. I built up in over 18 months or so, scaled and sold that one for another very nice lump sum of a few hundred thousand US dollars.

I really felt I had this physical products formula and strategy in a rinse and repeat format. I knew what kind of products to look for. How to work with the suppliers and the supply chains and order those products, get them packaged and shipping into Amazon. I live in New Zealand, so I'm a long way away from most of the markets where I would buy physical products. That didn't matter when I could partner through Amazon. Amazon was pretty much the only platform I could run a business like that.

A slightly different e-Commerce business model is to "drop-ship" products. I could send customers to my websites, they would place an order and then I would place the same order with my supplier to ship the product directly to the customers. That's the beauty of drop shipping, you don't need to buy the product with your own money first. On Amazon I was running out of funds before running out of profitable product ideas. So dropshipping's cash flow had some appeal, but you had to be very aggressive and active with Facebook ads to make that work and the margin's got a bit tight too. So, I had a really good look around after selling two Amazon businesses, and then almost by accident I stumbled into generating my own information product.

INFORMATION PRODUCTS

The world of information products! They are another way to generate wealth and maintain a fantastic lifestyle from anywhere in the world. My first information product was probably the least efficient one, which was me selling my time coaching. I had picked hundreds and hundreds of different Amazon products, quit the day job and moved down to the south island of New Zealand and built a dream home. We were living the good life in the southern alps in a beautiful alpine ski town and people were asking how I did it.

How did I manage to quit my job, what was this business thing I was doing from home? And so, a bunch of people have asked me for some help. I talked to a few people for free, but what I also figured is when you help people for free, they tend not to value that teaching and help that you're giving them. They don't tend to do much with it. I had seen a lot of people setting themselves up as Amazon coaches and I'd paid for some private Amazon coaching, and paid a lot of money for it.

I could see that if I charged a handful of people an hourly rate like that for some one-on-one coaching, then it would just top up my income stream and it meant I wasn't quite so reliant on my Amazon products. The other thing that happened at the same time when I was thinking about starting coaching was I could see some of the products that I was buying myself at home, in New Zealand. I had young children at the time, so there were a few New Zealand owned brands, family businesses, that had great quality products that was so good I wanted to sell them on Amazon myself.

I knew those products would stand out in the market. They were high quality and unique. Just the sorts of products I would source and sell myself. But with these ones, I thought maybe I could do it slightly differently. Maybe instead of me buying the products from Asia or even New Zealand to ship and sell on Amazon, maybe I could do a consulting model where for a monthly retainer, I look after those companies businesses on Amazon. I would set up their Amazon account for them, run it and report back monthly. Run all the day to day stuff myself and generate some extra income by offering a service from home.

In business you're either selling products or services. I was good at selling products and this was my first venture into selling services. Coaching Amazon sellers on which products to pick and then running a service helping New Zealand companies by selling their products for them on Amazon. That would generate more sales and more profit for them and I would charge a monthly retainer or some kind of commission.

I got started and I did both coaching and consulting much in parallel. I got my first coaching client, who was a lovely girl from Hawaii. She did a really nice product. I introduced her to my designer, who did a great job with the private labelling and creating her brand. At the same time, I approached four companies who were local businesses near where I lived and said, "Would you like me to look after your products for you on Amazon? I'm sure they'll be popular, and if not, it's a pretty cheap experiment, and I'll do all the work. If it works, then we'll share some of the revenue being generated."

Four out of four of those companies said, "Yes!" So, I was off to my first consulting gig and also my first coaching client. Off I went. I'd been used to working from home. I'd set myself up with a small home office space, pretty much at the kitchen table while the children were at daycare. Then I shifted out to the garage and converted some of that to office space, because once I was doing coaching, I had to do calls in private and not be interrupted by the children or have the normal household racket going on in the background.

While I'd been able to do my products business in the main home, I decided to get a bit more professional. I set up a separate space to do my calls and the consulting and coaching work. After about a year, I had a very full calendar of coaching clients who were paying me a lot of money for one-on-one help. I also had some consulting clients who had some great products selling and through the monthly payments that they made to me as my monthly retainer, I was able to hire somebody to run the day to day admin on my accounts and my clients' account.

I had a virtual assistant who I hired online from Canada, and I was up and away. I had my own products selling on Amazon, I had coaching clients, and I had consulting clients. It turned out that the consulting clients were quite high maintenance. I would do what I would do on my own Amazon products, but still there were a lot of emails, and phone calls to deal with. It wasn't really going to scale, because even though I had some help with the administration of those accounts, the clients really wanted to deal with me direct when they wanted to hear what we were doing to grow sales each month. Things such as how to interpret what was happening on the statistics, how things were tracking, how we were going to keep increasing sales, or launch new products, and the same with the coaching clients.

It was very hard for me to outsource that. They really wanted to deal with me one-on-one, especially for the investment they had made. They wanted my insight as to which products were good ones for them to sell on Amazon. There were good things and bad things there. One of the good things was that it was great cash flow. It meant I didn't have any pressure on the Amazon product side of the business. All my profit from my Amazon products, I plowed back into more Amazon products, which was great.

I launched over 400 Amazon products in my first year like that. The other thing that I noticed was my calendar was getting full. Now I'd given up my day job to have more freedom, but in the end I would wake up and see my calendar for the day and there'd be three or four coaching calls booked in. An hour of really intense one way energy of me coaching other people.

That was fine. It was good and interesting work. It was stimulating, they were great clients, and nice people who wanted to do well. I wanted to help them. But it couldn't scale. I was pretty tired after I did those calls. They're very intense and I only had so many hours in the day. I figured out I bought myself another job. It was very lucrative, but it was really fixed to that hourly rate that I could charge and how many hours I was willing to work in a day, or a week on other people's businesses rather than my own.

At that stage, I decided to stop and have a think about what I could do it differently. I'm giving you this full story, start to finish about what I've done over the last five years. Because we're going to dive deeper into all of these different business models, into Amazon, into coaching and consulting, and the next one, which is online courses.

When I was coaching my Amazon clients, who were looking for help with choosing products, I found myself repeating myself a lot. I would go through the criteria that I looked for in products, the process was exactly the same each time, but the criteria and the decision making around which products were good ones was very repetitive. I'd spend at least half of the 10 coaching calls repeating myself. It was very one way, me downloading what I figured out, what I liked and didn't like with different types of products. Which categories of products were good, what features of a product were good, what to avoid. How to work with suppliers, all the shipping and set up, which outsourcing experts I used for branding or copyrighting.

I was sharing all the same stuff over and over again, at a very high price but very inefficiently really, because I was doing it all myself. So, what I thought I would do was once I had a bunch of these coaching clients, maybe charge them less but put them in a group together and turn it into a group course. I would record some modules for them, and then also give them some group coaching, so they got to learn from each other too. They got to be part of a community of people who could trust and talk about our products. Generally people don't in the Amazon world, they tend to be very secretive about which products they sell.

It was really nice to have a small group of like minded people selling on Amazon, working together, helping each other out, following my strategy for which products to sell, but implementing it together. That changed the game, because suddenly I could take on groups of 10 people and I would do a couple of one-on-one sessions with them to really do some brainstorming and strategy individually. All the process stuff flowed on from there. We could get much more efficient where they learned how to do barcodes, or which questions to ask suppliers. I didn't have to repeat myself. They could watch a training module that I recorded once and follow that. Download the question transcripts, download the spreadsheets to calculate Amazon fees or shipping fees, all those things that go into calculating whether a product is a good one or not, and how to launch it.

I got to a real turning point there by realizing that I didn't just need to sell my time hours for dollars. I could create an information product and sell that. So, after a couple of intakes of group coaching, I stopped all the one-on-one coaching. I would still give everyone doing the group coaching and the online course some private one-on-one time, but I really flipped the model around to be scalable.

At that stage, I hired my own business coach. I'll talk more about coaching later and how to become a coach. Getting my own coach was a really good investment and I still work with her today. Every year I buy a big block of hours and we work together. We partner with some things and she coaches me on other things. That's been a really smart investment, having the skills to find my own clients online and deliver a program to them online as well. This is about year four, I've done Amazon products, Amazon consulting, Amazon one-on-one coaching, and then Amazon group coaching and an Amazon course.

The Amazon course was still a big investment for people. They were getting an intensive experience, they were still getting some one-on-one time and I wondered if instead of people paying about $5,000 for that, whether I'd make a decent profit and be able to scale even further by really lowering the cost of the basic training. Then reserving the one-on-one time and the more intensive coaching for the smaller number of people that wanted that additional personal support.

Once I scaled the group coaching and there were more people wanting to do that, I decided I would launch an online subscription model. The idea was to create a recurring revenue stream and with my coaching clients, I would recruit them. I would have a call with them to decide if it was right for them, and if we were going to work well together. They would pay me, I would do the coaching, and they would do the work and off we went. Then, when we got to the end that was it.

The world of Amazon is always changing and they wanted to stay in touch, keep up to date and wanted to hear what else I was doing. What I thought I could do is once a week, do a live webinar to everybody who was in an "inner circle" who had coaching with me, and I'd just share what's working in e-Commerce and on Amazon. Keeping everyone up to date with what's happening, what's working and what I'm learning. Also what I'm figuring out, what's changing on the platform, what's happening more broadly in the world of e-Commerce like how to run Facebook ads or hire a virtual team.

I was learning a lot of stuff that I was willing to share and I enjoy teaching. I had a lot of students who wanted to learn, but not everybody had the level of investment available that they would need to get that really intense experience, so I set up a subscription model that's called, Product University. That still runs now and every single Friday morning I teach live for an hour. At the very beginning, people could sign up for this for $97 a month, and they would get the full Friday live sessions plus they'd get the online Amazon course, and they wouldn't get any one-on-one time from me.

There was zero time commitment from me for every new client that came along and joined that model. This was probably the best thing I've done. I still run that model today, it really suits me because I love teaching, sharing what works and I love learning. When I have to teach something, it gives me the chance to learn it. Really understand it, digest it, teach it and share it. Product University has been really good, because it's led to a recurring income stream. Every member that joins stays a member and that revenue just keeps rolling in from my point of view, and then from their point of view they get the ongoing up-to-date Amazon and eCommerce training.

I've gone much broader than just Amazon. I've been teaching people how to build virtual teams, do branding online, source from different countries, go to trade shows and find products, how to do Facebook ads, YouTube ads and all the different things that help you run an online business.

I really enjoyed setting up something that was a lighter touch, but could reach more people and be affordable to more people. Now I've got quite a few thousand members in that program, who signed up and every week get the live Friday Product University update that I teach. That was a really good model that worked really well for me. It was a game changer because it meant I was not doing anymore one-on-one coaching. My own Amazon products were great and I was doing lots of experiments to test things and discover things, I was able to teach what worked.

A business partner who I'd work with on the consulting side of the business took over all the clients there, because that didn't really work well for me. I did it with young children and living at the bottom of the South Island of New Zealand. If they wanted me to be at a meeting in Auckland on the North Island, or preparing papers for boards, it was just a different style of work that didn't really suite the lifestyle I was after. It was definitely lucrative, there was definitely a demand for the skills and the service but it wasn't something I really wanted to focus on. So my business partner took over that side of the business and I exited and focused on my Amazon products and teaching Amazon best practice to all the people that wanted to listen.

That was a successful model that really showed me that you can make a lot of profit by selling information products, not just physical products. The information product world then opened up for me. Over the next few chapters, I want to share with you a whole bunch of things about the world of information products, because it's a really different way to working from say the corporate career, or working in a products business.

There's some wonderful things about information businesses. One is that they're very lean. You can be very frugal and set these things up at fairly low cost. Once the content has been created, it's good profit margins on sales if you're selling an online course, or even a book. Something like that you create once, but then you sell for profit again, and again, and again, without having the high cost of goods that you have with physical products.

One of the other nice things about information products is that you can do everything working from home, which is great. You just need to have wifi and be online for a few hours a day. I'm probably only working an hour or so a day at my desk at the moment and that home based lifestyle really suits me, so it can be very informal. You could choose to go to a co-working space if you enjoy that environment, but I actually prefer just working from home. When I want to socialize or see people I go and do that around my own interests and passions, rather than around my work.

The other thing about working from home and having an information product business is you get really good at being productive by managing your time and energy. You can be productive and create a lot of new content. Stay up-to-date by learning and teaching, or learning and writing, or learning and coaching. Whatever it is that your information product's around, you can be very productive. It certainly doesn't need to be a full time job to earn at least what you would have earned, in your full-time 9:00 to 5:00 traditional style of work.

One of the other neat things about an information product business, is that you can do a lot of it where you are masterminding and creating this strategy and the big picture. The game plan of your business. There's a lot of help that you can hire online, and you never even often meet these people, but there's some really skilled labor and very low cost labor that can help you finish producing your online products. Whether it's a graphic designer who designs the front cover of an eBook, or a video editor who makes your online course look great, or a virtual assistant who runs your Facebook ads for you, you don't need to do everything yourself.

You can run a small but very efficient, relatively low cost team and really scale your business without having a huge staff headcount. Just a bunch of very specialized freelancers who are the best at what they do, and are just there on demand as you need them to help you grow your business and deliver whatever your product is. I've really enjoyed having an online team. I've got one part-time operations manager who helps coordinate a lot of the different projects I've got on the go. Then everybody else is just a freelancer on an agreed hourly rate.

There's somebody doing design work, somebody doing sourcing work, or somebody doing a transcription. For example, even this book I dictated and then I used a website called Rev.com to transcribe it to text, which is very low cost. Then I edited what came back for the written version.

The production side can be done at low cost, by getting freelancers or virtual teams helping you do what you need to do. There's also a really nice thing with information product businesses, is that you can be based anywhere in the world. They're generally location independent. If you want to be on the beach in Bali, which is where I was for three months with my Amazon business. Or you may want to live in a small ski town where there's no jobs, which is where I live now, a very small 6,000 person town in the south island of New Zealand. Apart from the hospitality and the ski industry, and a little bit of wine industry work, but certainly nothing like I used to work as a diplomat in the city.

The beauty of just being able to live where you want is amazing and the cost of living outside of main centers is so much lower. You can live in Southeast Asia, where the cost of living is very low, but you can have a real five star lifestyle. There's a lot of digital nomads in places like Chiang Mai in Thailand, having a great quality of life and having a healthy lifestyle, while running really smart online businesses.

At the end of this introductory chapter, I just wanted to make sure that you've got a feel for how the world of information products is very variable, and I also want to make it really clear that everybody's path through this will be very different. I like to have a private life and so social media's not really for me. I don't have an Instagram account, I don't do Facebook. I run Facebook ads, but I don't spend any of my time broadcasting my life. My personal time is mine and it's very private. I don't share photos of my children on the internet. I just live a very quiet life.

I ride my horse, I go skiing, drop my kids to school and pick them up. I do some coaching and teaching work, Amazon work, products, managing all my online projects for a few hours a day, or a few hours a week, maybe only an hour or two a day.

When I am working I'm very productive. I've got help delivering it through my virtual team, and then when I'm not working, I'm completely relaxed and at home. I don't need to have that over spill of office politics or people contacting you outside of hours. It's a really neat business model where you control what comes through to you, what comes through to your inbox, or what gets handled by someone else. Even what work you do and don't do. You are completely in control.

I think I was born fairly entrepreneurial and always wanted to do my own thing. When I was working at the university, raising venture capital funding for startup companies, I could see that there was a huge amount of cash that was burnt through before the proof of concept was even established. There was a timeline of five or 10 years of research and development to get the product ready for market. I like to see things happen a little bit faster than that and I didn't like how long it took to see these projects come to fruition.

There were lots of exciting milestones along the way, but I could see for me and the kind of lifestyle that I like, I didn't need to make tens of millions. I just wanted to not have to work really hard for somebody else. I wanted financial freedom and independence. I wanted to have a business that I was really proud of. I've always created products and services that suit me. What I want to do in the following chapters is to help you understand what else is out there. How these online courses work, how webinars work, how sales funnel work, how social media marketing works and how you can start a service business from home. Selling your time, or selling an online information product that will give you that financial freedom and independence as well. You too could potentially generate 6 or 7 figure income streams from information products when you know the right way to do it and get the right help.

Not all of these information product business models suit everyone and I've always really enjoyed physical products, Amazon products are fun for me. I find that comes quite naturally and quite easily. I can go to a trade show and spot products that I know will sell well on Amazon. If I had a business where I was running somebody else's Google analytics on their advertising campaigns or something like that, I would be cross-eyed and climbing the walls. That detailed, data driven analytical work doesn't really suit how I think or my temperament. I don't get to use my creative skills, it's much more analytical and detail focused. Whereas I much prefer creative and big picture kind of projects.

We will spend some time in this book, helping you become more self aware of your personality and your skills. Where those skills and that temperament will best sit in the world of information products, so you can start focusing on the areas and the business models that suit you.

The key part of the book is to go through all the different business models out there. Some people might be great at writing and broadcasting ideas. Some writing great articles or blog posts. Sharing stuff on social media to raise a following and get an audience listening to you. Or, following your recommendations and advice and looking to you as an authority or an influencer in your space. That's things like affiliate marketing. There's people who've got great analytical skills who could run things like advertising agencies, or run other people's campaigns for Amazon adverts, Facebook or Google ads for more numerical and data driven projects. You need to use your skills to create a product or service, then market it to monetise it.

The more passive you can get that income stream the better, as then you're out of the hours for dollars trap and can really scale and generate real wealth.

There are people who are great with people, so if you enjoy coaching, we'll show you how to set up a coaching business or an online course. This is even more efficient and scalable, because you only create the content once and then you've still got the ability to work one-on-one with those people that want the individual coaching. It's the 80/20 rule. You've shared 80 percent of the good stuff in a course. Then you can do the more advanced final 20 percent with people in a different format.

We'll also have a look at products businesses. We'll look written content such as eBooks or articles. Generating those and building a business through being good at creating content. We'll also have a look at eCommerce. An eCommerce business is things like a Shopify store or a Woo Commerce. Any website where you're selling products and running adverts on Facebook or YouTube, to get customers over to your website to order your product. It might be products that you've got sitting in a warehouse, or they're just drop shipped straight from the manufacturer as you receive the product order.

There are lots and lots of different ways out there to sell your products or services online. We'll look at the model around sales funnels, which is a really neat way to introduce a potential customer to your product and to you. Then to help build that knowledge and trust between the two of you before you make an offer for your product or services for sale. Sales funnels have changed the game for online business. They've made it a logical ascension from being complete strangers online to doing business together online.

The way sales funnels are put together has really changed the numbers around people's willingness to buy a product they don't know online. It builds trust and it helps educate people before they're asked to part with their money and invest in the product or service. Whether you're selling any kind of product or service, sales funnels are a really important thing for you to understand in this world of online business. In the Freedom Navigator course, I teach people how to build sales funnels that automate marketing and sell their product or service.

I want to share a little bit about my philosophy. As you know, I was really motivated to go into business of my own, because I wanted more freedom. I wanted to not be working hard for somebody else in a day job, coming home exhausted and then my own family getting the leftovers. The shattered and depleted version of me who'd been working hard elsewhere all day and all week. I really wanted to build something that set me up to be free and to live where I want and to put my family first. Then to have an efficient business, that generated enough income to live really well.

I hadn't expected the level of success I've had and I've had it across different products and services businesses. I'm going to share what they are in more detail in the rest of the book. But, some of the philosophical thinking behind the business, in all that I've started, is they've had some similarity. All of them have been done on a shoestring. I've never gone into debt for any of these businesses and I've often partnered to create opportunities in areas that I don't have the expertise.

I've been very frugal, so I keep everything as simple as I can for as long as I can. I don't go for really fancy high profile complicated business models. I like simple until they're proven, and then I can expand from there. I like to keep everything under the radar, so my own personal profile is not what sells my products or services. The content does, which means it's much easier to scale and to partner with other people.

For example, my Amazon training program, I partnered with a marketing company in Australia who've now taken that global. I created the content once, they do the ongoing marketing. I keep delivering the training, keep all the content up-to-date and do the live weekly sessions. But the global expansion, that is something that I would not have been able to do myself without seriously investing in Facebook ads and going into debt and learning about areas that weren't my natural area of expertise. There's no way I would be good at running seminars if I knew nothing about seminars, but I partnered with a seminar company who got my product out in front of people.

Partnering and working with the right people in the right way is absolutely essential. As well as investing in your own coaching, learning and development, so I do a lot of reading. We've got a whole chapter on learning and development and the key business books that I think all eCommerce and online entrepreneurs should be aware of and read most of them. I'll share with you which ones I think are the best and for which topics. I've also really focused on being productive, so I try to keep everything as lean as possible, spend as little as possible, test the market with the very basic version and then improve it based on feedback.

In the software game that would be known as developing the minimum viable product, I like to do a soft low cost launch, get some feedback and then scale up from there. I've really made sure that all the businesses I start are things that I'm proud of, things that I enjoy. If I was forcing myself to do detailed analytics of a spreadsheet of my cost per click everyday, I would be a miserable person. It brings me joy taking people around the world on trade shows, visits to Vietnam and India to find products to sell on Amazon or their websites. It's great fun, great travel and adventure meeting wonderful people.

What you'll learn in this book is all the different information and online business models that are out there. By the end you'll have a much better idea of the pros and cons of each of those, and a good feel for which ones will fit you with your skills and personality. I'm really looking forward to sharing it all with you. We're going to be covering a wide range of topics. We'll be looking at; mindset, productivity, virtual teams, how to automate your business and all the technology and tools that exist to help eCommerce entrepreneurs run smart online businesses in a way that's scalable and profitable.

We'll be looking at all the different business models. So that's the bulk of the book, all the different business models that you can run online. Information products that you can run as an eCommerce entrepreneur from home, whether it's a piece of software, or a coaching business, or writing articles, whatever it is that suits you, we'll show you how to make money with that skill. We'll be looking at things like partnerships and how to grow your business, because not all scaling is done by you with your own funds. You might find ways to scale that are through alliances or partnerships, affiliate partnerships or other businesses that align well with you and can take you places that you couldn't go on your own.

We'll have a look at things like social media and we'll have a look at one exciting topic at the end as well, which is selling your business. One of the traps with information products is that if it's all about you or if it's only you that can deliver that skill or service, then it can be very hard to sell that business. If I was just doing my one-on-one Amazon coaching, I wouldn't be able to sell that business very easily because the new owner would still need me to deliver all the coaching. But, some businesses like my Amazon businesses, I've sold two of those, and online course businesses, education businesses, they can be sold. Affiliate sites can be sold, drop shipping and eCommerce sites can be sold.

We will go through the pros and cons of selling a business, which is a really exciting game changer. I've had a couple of really big paydays through businesses I've started from home that have let me pay off an entire mortgage, build a new house and make significant lifestyle changes. Selling a business is where we'll finish, but we'll start with where to begin and we'll always make sure that these businesses aren't just creating yourself another job. We don't leave our day jobs and take on the extra risk and pressure of being a business owner to work as many hours and for less return than we did in our day job.

We want to be working smarter, not harder. We want to work hard, but we don't want to end up creating ourselves another 60 odd hour a week job. The Four Hour Work Week by Tim Ferriss is probably the book that got me on this track and starting to think about smart business models Ways to be entrepreneurial and have a successful mix of lifestyle and profitable business. That philosophy of being very lean, efficient and scalable is really important, and so in all the different business models I'll be showing you a model that really works on part-time hours.

That's neat in two ways, once it's up and running, you've got freedom but also short-term, you can keep your day job while you set these up. You don't need to quit what you're doing at the moment to get this thing up and running. I really recommend for your first business, you don't quit the day job too soon. It's going to be a bit harder to find the hours, but it will give you a lot more security to let you grow and scale a lot faster. If you have an extra income stream backing you up while you make a start as an online business owner, it reduces your risk.

I'm really looking forward to diving into these other topics with you. It's going to be a fast, flying visit through all the different business models and we'll also show you where you can go to learn more about each one. Whether you're interested in starting an agency for PR or for advertising, whether you want to become a business coach, or whether you want to promote other people's products and just get the commission because you've generated the sales from home. All while you've been living the lifestyle you want, these different business models have pros and cons and we'll show you how you can also go on and learn much more detailed ways of launching and implementing these different business models.

There's about half a dozen different business models we'll look at in this book, and at the end of the book you'll find out more about how to progress if you are ready to get started with one of them. So, welcome! Congratulations on finishing the first chapter. I'm really looking forward to helping you find your own track to financial freedom.

LEARNING AND DEVELOPMENT

One of the things that I've done consistently, that has really paid off in my business, has been always making sure I stay at the front of the pack in terms of what's working and making sure I understand the principles of the business. In all the different business models, there's always the fundamentals. The principles, the reasons why somebody would come along and buy your product and service, the principles of marketing, the principles of doing successful business, making a profit and having a sustainable business, and having a business model that's smart and scalable and sustainable.

But there's also the tactical stuff. I see a lot of people ducking and diving, trying to chase the latest tactical stuff without investing in their learning to understand the really important fundamentals of business. What I want to do in this chapter, is to share with you some of the most important books and learnings that I've had along the way. The times where I've invested in myself and how that's paid off.

The very first thing was not an investment of my own dollars, but my own time. I was working for the university and they funded me to do an MBA. I completed an MBA at the full-time speed while I was working a full-time job. Completing four papers a semester and four semesters in one year. That was 16 papers on top of a full-time job as a manager in the university. It was a full-time job. It wasn't a full-time plus plus job like some of the other ones I'd had a bit later. I was in my mid-twenties. I was really ambitious and motivated to do well at work, and had the opportunity where the chair of my board offered to invest in me to do an MBA.

I could have completed it half-time over two years, which is what nearly everyone else did. But I really wanted to push on. I like the feeling of getting things done and I did a few things together. One was I did an accelerated study skills course. There's a lady called Karen Boyes in New Zealand who has a course on study skills. She came and presented a weekend session with us on speed reading and training your memory, as well as some habits for studying and habits for managing your energy. It was just fantastic. There were rapid fire techniques to become a better learner and that really helped me. Whenever I've signed up for somebody's online course, I was able to cut to the bits that matter. I could read the material fast as downloads rather than watching hours and hours of videos.

I could make mind maps to understand how things all came together in the structure and the most important points of something I was trying to understand or learn. That accelerated study skills training was fantastic and it's something I teach my own students now. Then the MBA itself was quite an interesting experience. There's an international standard. The standard MBA with 16 papers on everything from accounting and corporate finance through to managing change and leadership and everything in between, such as operations and economics. All the kind of hardcore business subjects. I really enjoyed it. I found passing the exams easy, partly because of the study skills. I came out of the MBA with distinction, and I realized that I wasn't necessarily the brightest in the class, but I'd got really good at doing assignments fast, reading fast and learning how to pass the exams with high marks.

I had high grades and ended up with a distinction, and it was a really good feedback loop because it gave me a lot of confidence that even with subjects I knew nothing about, I could learn them pretty efficiently, master them well enough to get by and do so quickly. That was really reassuring because my first degree was in science, so all the subjects like corporate finance were unfamiliar to me and looked daunting when we were looking at things like Black Scholes formulas for valuing shares. But you learn it once and put it into practice, do a few practice runs of the exam paper, read a few textbooks and away you go.

The MBA was fun but the best thing I got out of that was learning how to learn, becoming a good learner. One thing I've noticed with people that do my own courses and programs is that they often don't take value out of the most important bits and they get lost in the weeds and start flapping around in the Facebook group about some tiny detail while they've missed the big picture.

With most things in life, the 80/20 rule generally applies. 80% of the benefit is gained from the first 20%, then you could spend ages and ages learning the last 20%, but it doesn't actually get you that much further. Master the basics and that's generally all you need. Whereas some people miss the 80%, find one little detail in the remaining 20% and really get themselves all worked up over that.

I run a couple of Facebook groups for my own coaching clients and for people studying Amazon with me. I see people who aren't getting the best value by studying the strategy and understanding the big picture. Instead they're worried about some little technicality that doesn't even apply to them yet because they don't need to decide which logo or website hosting service they need. They just need to choose the first product that suits Amazon. The logo or domain provider isn't what's going to make or break their business, but they latch onto something that they can control that isn't actually that important.

One of the important things with learning and how to be a good learner, is working out what matters in each subject. If you're learning about how to be an affiliate marketer, then certain stats and performance metrics on the products that you're looking to promote matter and a format for how to write great emails, that stuff really matters. But some of the other things are far less relevant. You could spend weeks and weeks fine tuning, but they won't make a big difference to the bottom line or your overall success.

Similarly, for something like an agency doing social media content for clients, you need to pick the right platforms and which bit of software you use to schedule the posts. You could research that for a very long time and of diminishing returns. They all pretty much do the same job. There's some personal preference and you want to choose one that works, but the strategy is what content to put out and on which platforms, not which bit of software should you agonize over using to schedule the posts.

Sometimes I see people getting lost and then often grinding to a halt because they've latched onto a detail and missed the big picture. Learn how to become a good learner. When I teach all my online training courses, I do a whole module on how to be a good learner and how to get the most value out of the courses. There's a lot of content in the courses and it's structured in a sequential way so you start at the beginning and do each step.

But if you don't implement each step as you watch a training video, it's hard when you've got to the end and go back and remember what video one told you to do. It's much better to be very action-oriented as you do training or do an online course. Make sure you put the work into practice at each step. It's harder work and you have to make decisions. But it's how you make progress, learn and get results. If, on my Amazon course, step one is all about opening your Amazon account and the action at the end of module one is to open an Amazon account, open it. Don't wait until you've ordered a product six months later and then you've got to go and watch all the videos again, it feels like you're going around in circles. Whereas you could've just gone step-by-step and be at the end by then.

Learning how to learn is really important, and learning who to learn from is also important. There's some really big names and it's not always the case that the biggest names have the most value to share. Some of the people that I've found have enduring and high quality original thinking. I've always listened to and followed and always respected their opinions in business or in life.

One of the best ones is Tim Ferriss. He's just a lifelong learner. He interviews people on success. He wants to find those short cuts and clues to success that people who've been successful in business or sport or whatever industry he interviews them for on his podcast. Tim Ferris is the master of hacking the fastest to learn and be successful at things. If you haven't read the 4-Hour Workweek, I highly recommend that. That's a really good book. Not just on different ways to earn money in a short space of time, but just how to think and how to learn. He's got a really refreshing approach, compared to sort of the more corporate inefficient way of getting things done in a business. Tim Ferriss is wonderful.

Somebody from a totally different background is Ray Dalio. He wrote a book recently called Principles, as he retired from his career as an investment banker. He's managed billions of dollars in his funds and he's just a smart and honest guy. What he's seen across all sorts of different industries, across the decades are really good lessons for business. I'll put all of these reading recommendations in an appendix for you as a reading list at the back of this book. But Ray Dalio's book on principles, if you follow those in business, whatever your business, if it's an agency or an online course or a content marketing freelance job, whatever you do, if you follow those principles, you won't go wrong.

Some of the other books that I really like and think are really good are some of the Richard Koch books, 80/20 Marketing. Perry Marshall, as well has written some great books on the Star Principle. That idea that you get 80% of the benefit from 20% of the work. That's true for most things in life and certainly in business. If you get the big picture right, the details will just follow or they're not that critical to your success.

A modern one is DotCom Secrets. This is a book by Russell Brunson and if you want to understand and actually spook yourself a bit when you realize how many times you've been on the receiving end of these sorts of sales funnels, is to understand the concept of the sales funnel. Russell Brunson developed software called ClickFunnels and it takes people from an initial Facebook ad through to a page where they might register their name and email address to download an ebook or something like that. Then they might be invited to watch your webinar. Then they might be invited to buy your short course. Then, maybe there's an up sale and they're invited to order a bonus package or an extended version or a coaching call or something like that. Over a sequence that's all delivered, of course, completely automated and completely online without the business owner being involved personally at all. They can sell their own products or services to their customers, 100% automated and 100% online.

Every e-commerce entrepreneur needs to really focus and study the DotCom Secrets book by Russell Brunson. He also launched a followup book called Expert Secrets and both of those are really worth reading to understand how a lot of e-commerce and online businesses can be marketed and the products and services sold all completely automated online. That's a really good read. Easy reading, well-written and if you haven't come across that book yet, that will really change your perspective on what's possible with online businesses. There are some motivating case studies in there as well, you can see what's possible with really simple products and services just being marketed through a sales funnel.

Another really great book to make sure you've read at some stage is Rich Dad, Poor Dad. This is Robert Kiyosaki sharing the principles to growing wealth. All of our businesses are capable of generating cash flow and they should all be generating profit. But there's also a shift in your financial education and understanding of principles about how money works and how tax works. It's told as a very engaging story. It's a very easy read. But Rich Dad, Poor Dad is really good for making sure you've really grasped what's important about growing wealth rather than just having money spin around. Turnover's fine, but you really want to be building assets, not having just a bunch of liabilities and growing how robust your portfolio of assets is over time. Rich Dad, Poor Dad by Robert Kiyosaki, is also on the list.

There's a bunch more. I'll put them all in the reading list at the back because some will appeal to some of you more than others. Learning how to write good copy is always a really valuable skill. Dan Kennedy's, is the master of writing sales copy and wrote, 'The Ultimate Sales Letter'. Other books that you might want to consider reading The Power of Habit by Charles Duhigg. We've got a whole section coming up soon. A whole chapter coming up soon on habits and habits for success as an entrepreneur. But the Power of Habit has been a best selling book by Charles Duhigg and it really breaks down what we can do to control our habits and make sure that the way we spend our time in our daily routines and things that we do on autopilot to support our business or our health or whatever it is that we're trying to influence and grow.

By having the right habits, it's much easier just to have a lot of that growth or success happening on autopilot without us having to work really hard at making it happen each day. It's a bit of an effort to create a habit, but once it's formed, that really makes a difference to what's possible in your life. Getting that tailwind and building a business with the right habits and the right lifestyle to support your business and the business to support your lifestyle. A lot of that's done by setting up habits and routines the right way. There's lots of great books, and you'll see the rest of those in the reading list.

Now also on learning and development, there's a bit of a trap which we often in the industry call shiny object syndrome. Once you are an Amazon seller your, every third post on our Facebook feed seems to be an ad for some other course or some too good to be true sounding bit of software. Maybe it's a webinar that you're being invited to watch. There's lots and lots of ongoing free or not free things that you can do to keep learning.

There's got to be a balance here because there's some very smart marketers who will have a steady stream of offers and will be courting you with these offers very convincingly to help you grow your business. They know what words and what triggers to use around the areas you're going to be struggling with. They will turn up in your feed on YouTube ads and Facebook ads, in your inbox, and there's a high risk of getting distracted by doing too much of chasing the shiny new things, rather than implementing the stuff that's fundamental and you've already got.

If you're starting a Facebook ads agency, the key things to do are get some clients and get good at running Facebook ads. You'll probably see some ads for how to run Google ads or how to pitch for consulting jobs or something like that. You could do consulting jobs, but really you're just doing one service. If you do that well, that's all you need to do. Often by getting spread too thin and too distracted you end up doing nothing well.

You feel overwhelmed. You feel financially stretched because you've invested in lots of different things, rather than just getting a good return on the first investment and the opportunity that it was all about. When things get hard, it is easy. The grass often looks greener and it often feels easy to jump onto a different horse that you'd want to go back and ride for a while and see where that takes you. But often the best thing to do is to get that feeling of having mastered one thing, implemented it properly, got it to where you can get it on your own and then look to invest more from ongoing learning and development. It might be that a coach is a good way for you to master the more advanced aspects of a business that you're running. Maybe a few books, a few podcasts and an online course to get you up and running and started.

Then maybe there's a few specific things that you need to iron out and maybe a short burst with a really good coach would help you with that or maybe joining a mastermind. There's a lot of mastermind groups out there which are eye watering expensive. Some are worth it and some are not. I've done some really good ones. One with Roger Hamilton. I've done ones around Amazon. I've done a one with ClickFunnels with Russell Brunson. Some have been much better value than others. I won't go into those in detail from my own experience now because everybody's experience with them will be different. But you can spend an awful lot of money on masterminds. However, I don't think you need to do that in the first year of business.

Just get started and then when you find some like minded people or somebody who's a really clear leader in your field who you really look up to, the opportunity to get the most advanced or more personal support, then look at doing that later on. You don't need to do that right away. Just get up and running and spend that time implementing and getting the basics established, getting some wins, some runs on the board. That feeling that you've made progress and you've made your own business happen, then you've earned the right to get that high end help. But often people are going straight off to get a coach on day one or joining a big mastermind when they don't know the basics. It's a bit of a waste of money because you can't keep up with the rest of the group because you haven't mastered the subject yet.

Hopefully most of those people running masterminds screen and make sure that the quality of members is high and it's for advanced topics. It's really fun when you get to that level and you get to network with people that are successful, think differently and come from different backgrounds. It's a wonderful way to learn and have a lot of fun as well. Lots of traveling experiences, in person retreats or bootcamps to stop and really immerse yourself into your subjects, but don't do it too soon. Just make sure you've done the basics first before you jump into any advanced or expensive programs like that.

Now another way that's good for learning is listening to podcasts. This is wonderful because you can be commuting or doing jobs around the house and also listening to half hour episodes by people in your field, who interview others or have their own show and share tips on what's working. There's often a lot of great content shared. It's always really up to date and topical. Certainly for e-commerce, there's so many great podcasts that you can listen to, so I'll include in the reading list a bunch of those that you can enjoy, but there's people like Mike Dillard with the Mike Dillard show is a really good one.

Tim Ferriss' one is a great podcast. There's a whole bunch more and I'll let you pick and choose from the list in the back, which ones you might enjoy. But you can look them all up on iTunes or whichever podcast provider you use and find some free and really quality podcasts to tune into once or twice a week. You don't need to listen to lots, but it'll give you that feeling of ongoing learning and staying current while being up to date with what's going on in your field.

The one thing that's absolutely certain and is the only constant in business is that there will be change. What works as a Facebook ad strategy this year, won't work next year. Plus social media platforms that are hot now won't be so this time next year. Strategies for winning Amazon products will have different criteria later on. Rules will change, fees will change, compliance issues will change, tariffs will change. You need to stay up to date. Investing and staying up to date is essential. It's not just nice to do it, it's essential. Otherwise, you'll be caught out and left behind. If you're not moving forward, you're actually going backwards. There's no such thing as staying still in business, because if you're not doing anything to go forward, other people are and they're overtaking you.

You really need to take responsibility for your own learning and development. If you don't enjoy learning, then being a business owner might not be for you. If you find it a real struggle to maintain any interest in your field, then why do you want to run a business in that field? You're going to have to be at the front of the pack to do well, which means you're going to have to invest in learning and staying current and knowing what works, as that changes over time.

I found that people who enjoy learning do well in business, and people that resist learning or resist change find it very challenging to cope with all the changing demands of being a business owner. It's not just the learning, it's the whole attitude to being flexible, and there's always going to be change. Somebody might leave your team. The rules of the platform might change. The strategies might change. You might have a new competitor. All the things that will come up in your business life, you're going to have to need to figure out with your own brain. The way to have the best solutions in your brain is to make sure that you've been absorbing great information from the best thinkers in your fields, and that's not necessarily joining the big fancy masterminds. It can be just listening to podcasts, reading some good books, signing up to various email lists to stay up to date. Maybe go to a conference or two a year.

Conferences can be really good, depending on where you

live in the world. They can be a big investment to get to. If I lived in the States, I'm sure I'd go to a lot more than I do living in New Zealand. Conferences can teach you formal content, but also have amazing networking opportunities. The things that you learn in the hallways, corridors and the friends that you make can often be even more valuable than the content of the conference itself. There's a whole bunch of ways to learn. Reading books on the fundamentals, listening to podcasts in your fields, getting inspiration from people who've done well in business around you, going to conferences and having a coach. We'll have a whole chapter about working with a coach later on, but that's been something that's really been a great investment when I've made it each time.

You can also join a mastermind, which can be a little bit of an overkill in the first few months. But certainly as you get established, making a profit and you want to scale, then masterminds can be great. You can even have smaller groups and join some Facebook groups. Have some accountability partners, or at a more micro level, just partner up with other like minded people who want to figure things out, learn and keep each other sharp. It's always a good feeling when you know that you're up to date in your fields and you enjoy learning. Learn how to be a good learner. Make sure you process and go through all the content in the course and make sure that you dedicate the time. Make it one of your habits to invest in your own learning and development. If you don't do this for yourself, nobody else will.

It is, without a doubt, the single best investment you'll ever make in your business is investing in yourself and having a sharp mind. The skills, great contacts and good critical thinking skills, so that when the problem or challenge or opportunity arises, you know what to think about. What you can come up with is a new set of circumstances. Learning and development is something that is a real luxury and it's also necessary. It's time I really enjoy. I always look forward to doing a course or going to a conference. It keeps me sharp and I really liked that feeling of improving my game. Nobody will do this for you. It takes a bit of effort, but when you put the effort in, you get the best return possible. Enjoy learning and keep reading. Reading's definitely a critical success factor.

All the interviews with the leading CEOs, one thing they all have in common is that they read. Warren Buffett reads 300 pages a day. Bill Gates goes off for reading retreats for a couple of weeks a year, and all the serious leaders in business and all the really successful people have reading and ongoing learning as a habit. Otherwise, they're quickly out of the game, especially in e-commerce.

This game changes, so you need to have your fingers on the pulse and make sure that when there's changes coming your there. You know about them and you react and respond in the right way. Enjoy your learning and your learning and developing yourself will always give you so many more opportunities than someone who's stagnant and just waiting to copy somebody else's hacks or shortcuts. Understand the principles and then you can think of these things for yourself. Learning and development, absolutely vital to be a successful business owner. You've taken the right steps already by reading this book. Congratulations.

CHAPTER 4

OUTSOURCING

A really great thing about online businesses and info prod-uct businesses is that a lot of the help that you might need can be sourced really cheaply online. And when you've been used to a more traditional career where the cost of hiring is really high, the responsibilities of being an employer are very oner-ous. You've got to provide space, superannuation, training, on-boarding and holiday leave and all the things that employees demand. That's before they have any issues or get sick, don't show up or any of the other challenges with managing staff. A lot of these gave away, but you still get the benefit of having very specialized help to get done what needs to get done in your business. And there's some really great platforms that are very easy to find people to help you run your business.

When we look at something like freelancerdot.com, upwork. com or even fiverr.com for something simple like getting a background and a photograph of a product made completely transparent or completely white, it's a $5 project. If I was to

53

muck around learning Photoshop, I would drive myself potty. It would take me ages and I wouldn't do a very good job. It would distract me from more important things that are much better use of my time.

Richard Koch and Perry Marshall teach this principle really well with 80-20 marketing. The types of tasks that are ten or even a hundred dollar an hour tasks, should be outsourced as soon as your business can afford it. If there's some customer service or help desk type work, you can find individuals to do that, or you can pay service like Zendesk to manage your customer inquiries and chat on your website through that sort of service and that really frees you up. If you have to start dealing with tracking numbers or helping people with lost logins, all of that stuff's really painful, really low value, very repetitive, very draining. If it's negative, if it's people asking for refunds, that can really get you down.

It's really good just to have somebody taking care of all that general support type work around your business. You could have a generalist who you hire as a general virtual assistant. That's what I do. I've got one person who has access to pretty much everything apart from banking and she'll help me with my inbox. She'll help organize travel, help with projects, manage any other freelancers and she just keeps the whole show on the road. She's got a much better eye for detail than I do. I can focus on the big picture and new projects and learning and then the things I start, she can help finish up. She is able to get all the details squared away, everything signed off and place files managed really tightly. It's a really great partnership when you know who to hire.

One of the things in the profiling tool we have as part of

freedom navigator is really understanding your strengths. And it's no good hiring someone else just like you because you both love talking about ideas and big picture stuff. I'd have a great time working with another creative person all day, but we'd never finished anything. We'd start a million things and finish nothing. The kind of people I tend to hire are very detailed, structured, mechanically minded people who love process, who love finishing things, who love filing away that last document in the proper folder. All the things that I would be very bad at getting around to doing. I'm really focused on creating content and finding products to sell on Amazon, that kind of thing. I'm in my element, but give me a stack of shipping paperwork that I'm meant to file and send barcodes to the right suppliers and instructions for shipping and addresses, it would all go a little bit wonky quite quickly if there was too much of that going on because I'm just not naturally good at details.

I can do it, but I wouldn't be using my best skills and I wouldn't enjoy it. There's other people who are really efficient at it, who love that kind of work, who cannot be happier than when everything's squared away and tidy in place and finished neatly. I hire people that are really structured, organized, who like systems and processes and that offsets my slightly scatty approach to starting things. And then what I start, I can get really good help implementing and finishing properly.

You want to hire for complementary temperaments as well as skills. You need to really respect each other. Even though you've got very different backgrounds and training and person-alities, you only want to hire people who you really can connect with and respect each other. You can't be complete polar op-posites and expect to get on really well as a harmonious team. If I get someone who does admin for me but is really bossy and gets very demanding and waving clipboards at me and hurrying me up to do things, it gets my back up a bit because I'll get to the things that need to be done, but in my own time. And I manage my time and my energy so that I put my best time and work into creating new things and I need help finishing stuff off. So that's what I've learnt. I've found that people that work in banks or who've been trained to be paralegals have had really good detailed training. They'll have had some security checks and decent training, screening and some experience. If they've worked in a bank for a number of years, they will definitely have had good attention to detail be professional and honest. I like to hire people that have got some track record, but they don't necessarily need to have done exactly the task I'm going to give them.

I never hire Amazon virtual assistants to my Amazon business. I like to train people up the way I do things. I like people who are research assistants who are good at solving problems.

Someone with a bit of initiative is far more useful to me than somebody who needs their hand held every step of the way. Somebody who can solve a problem rather than send me a really long email explaining the problem, is by far the better hire. It might take a few goes online hiring people to find the perfect next person for your team.

In my online course I go through a bunch of questions, the scripts and some template job descriptions that you can use for hiring people in a team. In an Amazon business there's a few really obvious roles. There's customer service, product sourcing and product Admin. With a Facebook ad agency, you're going to need some analysts to help crunch the numbers as well as some creatives to do some pretty graphics and some marketing people to think of some great copy. Often these businesses will need a whole range of skills. While even the most talented generalists could do everything, it's not a good use of your time to everything yourself. Often those lower value jobs like customer service can be very cheaply outsourced and done well.

Graphic design is a good example. If you're not a designer, don't try and teach yourself design or photoshop and do your own logo. Just pay Looka.com, or find a graphic designer online to do your logo for you. You could work out how to write WordPress code and be a developer, but it could be a lot cheaper and better just to pay someone who's been doing it for years to really quickly and professionally do the job. Plus they'll see things that you haven't thought of and be aware of all the other bits that fit in around the exact brief that you've given them.

You're buying somebody else's experience as well as their skills so they can do the job, but they'll also, if they're the right kind of freelancer, be thinking about what you need as a client. They might make suggestions. They might challenge the brief, which is great. I love it when people are thinking for themselves and I might have just said, "Could you do this logo in yellow?" And they'd come back and go, "Well that'll look terrible printed on white paper. Yellow isn't a good color for a logo." So that's the kind of feedback I want before I've paid someone to do the logo in yellow.

There's some really talented people out there. It's a hirers' market. There's probably more people looking for work than offering work, which is great. So as a business owner you get the pick of some really capable people. They're all around the world. They're usually fast to turn work around, if they're hungry for more work. This week I've hired a bunch of different people on all completely unrelated tasks. I've had people helping me source products from India. I've had a profiling quiz turned into some software. A whole mishmash of different skills. I've had somebody helping design packaging.

Some of these things can be single short tasks. Some of them can be more ongoing projects. Some of them could be a retainer and somebody's just available two days a week to help you manage various projects that you give them. But over time your business will definitely need more than just you running it to scale. Accept that you're going to have to let go of some control. Apart from banking, which I never let anybody near, I've let go of pretty much every other part of my business. I've had other people write my Amazon listings. I've had other people manage my Amazon shipments. I've had guest coaches come in. I've had all sorts over the years as I've had to scale my business and let go of some of the bits that I started myself, but don't need to always do myself forever more.

It really liberates you when you find the right person and you see them hand in that first project that you give them and they've done a great job. It hasn't cost you very much and they want more work and you've got more things that need doing. It's a really great feeling when you realize just how capable some of these people are. Their hourly rates are often much lower than the cost of hiring them locally where you live. Certainly that's the case for me, but it's really just the flexibility. You just pay for the hours that you need or the length of task that needs doing. Just pay a one off fee, and it's done. And it keeps it really clean and there's even a bit of protection for you through services like Upwork. The freelancer doesn't get paid until they've done the work. And that hour tracking is done through some software as they work through the project, so they can't bill you for more than they've done.

It totally changes business ownership compared to the more traditional model. I'd say that a lot of design agencies or PR agencies should be really nervous given the quality and talents of all those people out there freelancing who can do just as good a job as those really expensive inner city ad agencies. There's no reason why the publications to promote your product need to be local in the city where that PR agents contact are. You can find a PR person on an online job site, say a freelancer, who can get your story written really well and pitched to all the right people in the industry worldwide. It gets very niche rather than localized, which is better because physical geographical location usually doesn't matter nearly as much as specialization. Online freelancers let you specialize and get the very best in the business to help you, whether it's design or copywriting, advertising, analytics, virtual assistance or just helping with admin.

It could be project managers or research assistants. All the jobs that you need to do to make all your ideas happen. You can really accelerate that progress by getting some help. Now all my new ideas, I rarely do the whole thing start to finish on my own. It's usually my idea and I start it off, and then I'll give someone a brief to research some competition or search some opportunities and come back with a summary. Then I'll go through that. Then I'll talk to some people. Then we kick it off as a proper project. Most of the projects I've got on the go now are run between about three of us and that's worked really well. Hiring outsourcing is one of the ways to scale your business. It's not expensive. It means the jobs done better, faster and cheaper than you doing it. And you can focus on your key strengths and the ideas and generating more business, then they can help you deliver what needs to be done.

I've shared in the appendix some of the sites that I like for hiring freelancers. Sometimes Tim Ferriss calls this the hug of death. He recommended a couple of agencies in India that do virtual assistance work, then they got so flooded by everybody using them at once, the quality of the service went down. I've only recommended some of the really big mainstream sites, but there are plenty of other specialized ones out there as well. Certainly once you get onto Fiverr, just look at the number of reviews, the number of successfully completed jobs, what level seller they are, and you'll get a good feel if it's somebody who is well established and going to do a quality job for you.

There's always the opportunity to do some toing and froing. What I personally find most annoying is that because you're going through these matchmaking sites, it's really hard to just get normal direct email from inbox to inbox. You've usually need to log into a Fiverr or Upwork platform to correspond with your freelancers. Over time it's usually better to have some help that's not going through those platforms for every bit of correspondence, but it's a great way to find people and just get one off jobs done. Enjoy the liberating feeling of hiring your first virtual assistant, building your virtual team and starting to outsource some of the tasks that don't come naturally to you, are low value and are just very specialized like design or web development. Things like that you just shouldn't be mucking around with trying to learn yourself, if you haven't got that background. Just get the help and get it right the first time.

Manage them tightly. Keep everyone honest, but you'll find you get a lot done for your budget when you find the right people in these specialist areas. Whatever kind of online business you have, there's a whole raft of people out there with all sorts of world class level skills who are looking for work and can help you do an even better job of building and scaling your business and deliver your service. So have a look at the websites I recommend and we'll see you in the next chapter.

CHAPTER 5

PRODUCTIVITY AND TIMEKEEPING

Productivity and managing your time well is an important factor in being successful when you've got any kind of business. Especially your own online business that you might run from home, because you're going to lack the structure of meetings and external deadlines that you might be used to from your previous day jobs. Suddenly it's down to you to face the awful tasks, the boring things like bookkeeping, difficult conversations that you can put off, decisions to make that involve spending money or investing in a product that you've been thinking about, or getting together to make the sales call and cold call a potential client. You've really got to be hungry for the results in order to push through to find and make the time to get your work done, but also to tackle the tasks that are going to make the biggest difference to your business.

I see a lot of people sit in a very comfortable zone of watching training videos and taking notes and maybe even getting quotes for products. They freeze when it comes to choosing the product itself and placing the order, wiring the money off to that new supplier for that new product, which then kicks off the whole stream of work, which leads to a sale. But without any product orders, they can't get any sales. The same with people selling services. If they are waiting for everything to be perfect before they can ring that first potential client for a sales call, get that first paying client, then it's going to be really difficult to build a business. So there's quite a lot of tools and tips out there to help us manage our time. Lots of high tech things, lots of books, apps, and philosophies.

I want to share some of the things that I've seen consistently work well. I think a bias towards action is always a winning approach to business, because there's a certain amount of theory that you need to understand. But after a point, you just need to get hands on, roll your sleeves up and get started with the real work. If it's choosing a product to sell through an e-commerce store, it may not be perfect. You may have a slight niggle that the competition might be a bit high or the demand might be a bit low, or the price might be a bit low, or the supplier hasn't been super responsive. All of these things aren't perfect, but I have launched nearly a thousand products and not one of them has been perfect and some of my million dollar products I almost didn't do, because I had a little niggle about them.

I'm really glad that over time, I've become confident making decisions to act, even though I've got imperfect information in front of me to make that decision. It's always a calculated risk. The benefit of launching a profitable product versus the potential loss if I invest in the wrong product. But there's ways to manage that. There's small product orders. When you're doing sales calls, you don't need to cover everything in the first call. You can introduce yourself, say "would you be interested in hearing more", maybe put the next thing in writing to them, and then sit down over coffee and go through some presentation or some numbers that you've run, or an offer that you've got. Go and do that face to face, or just break the format down to a style that suits you better. So if it's easier for you to do things by email rather than over the phone, that's fine.

Sometimes a Skype call for a sales call is actually nicer than a phone call, because with a bit more body language you can read the other person. It's a bit less bland and faceless. It's nice to be able to see somebody else's reactions and actually make eye contact as you have a conversation. It's much easier to build rapport, trust and close the sale. Also, being practical, there might be products to look at or websites to look at together on a shared screen, so I do like the format of just making eye contact and having conversations rather than hiding behind emails for too long.

It might be uncomfortable, but if you think you're going to run an agency and you're shy about getting on the phone to find clients, that's going to be a real problem. Likewise, if you've got difficult staff who aren't great and you need to let them go. If you can't face that difficult conversation to get rid of someone who's not performing, even if they're not employed, just a contractor or a freelancer, then you're going to be stuck with all sorts of quality problems. That will come back and be an issue from the client side later, or on your bottom line because they're not a productive staff member. You really need to just be a leader in your business and face those difficult decisions.

There's some very cool apps and tools to help people manage their time and productivity. One's called Pomodoro, which is a popular little tool that looks like a tomato and it's a timer that gives you 25 minute blocks of work. This is supposed to be the most productive little span to focus in on a particular task. Some people like to have apps on their phones, productivity apps or time tracking apps, or manage their to do lists. I use an app called Todoist and I share that with my team. I write my to do list as I'm out and about, jot things down. Some are personal, some are work things and then the team ones get shared. Other people in the team can jump onto them and get those underway, or I can assign them to named people in my team. I've looked at all sorts of really fancy software project management online. I've used Trello and Slack channels.

Actually the best thing that's worked, is having a small team of really high quality people who work fast and can keep up with me. We do most of our messaging through Skype, which is free. Just instant messaging, can attach files, can call each other, track the conversation which is searchable. You can use it off our phones and that's worked really well. If there's one tool that I probably couldn't live without, for managing the workflow of my team, it would be Skype. Funnily enough, which is not really what it's designed for, but that's just what's worked for me for five years now with pretty much every project has been run through Skype.

There are some documents of course, and I try and keep my office paperless. I've got no physical pieces of paper at all for my business apart from some accounts, which needs to be printed off for legal reasons and signed. But apart from that, everything is in the cloud. So I've got secure Dropbox folders for things like design files, contracts and invoices from suppliers, all the documents that support the business. I use Zoom for coaching calls and my live weekly webinars. We've got Dropbox for managing all the documents. We've got Skype for instant messaging and calling each other and there's no paper. It's very light and very minimalist, which is great. There's no expensive bits of software or any fancy tools, anywhere extra to log in or any extra places to go and find documents. Everything's just there at our fingertips.

One thing I know that works really well for getting the real progress on a project, is a great book called The 12 Week Year by Brian P. Moran. A book that's really all about getting your work rate up to kind of a sprint, as if you're doing the sprint finish at the end of the year when you're about to chase the year end, and get all those last minute deadlines closed. Hit the targets in your last little sprint finish of the year. Instead, he thinks we should all work like that all the time and set little sprints of 12 weeks throughout the year so we can have a break between them. You set a cracking pace by having really clear deliverables each week, detailed breakdown of what has to happen within each project against each week of the 12th week block. Then we get productive and that mode has really worked well for me and my team.

We're really fast. We really focus on big important projects, and the little stuff just doesn't clog things up. Whereas if you let the little things clog things up, you never get to the big important projects that you really want to happen. I've really found the 12 week year to be invaluable. I get all my coaching clients to do it and it really gets us off to a good cracking pace. If people have said, we're going to have launched our products or our services by week 12, then they worked backwards all the steps that they'll need to have done each week to hit that 12 week target. It really ups the ante and gets people working fast and it breaks things down. Each week is not some big, loose, intimidating, to do list. It's very clear, broken down steps and if you keep on track and keep up with those, then you'll hit some really big outcomes and big results. I've really enjoyed the 12 week year and how it makes me clear and productive.

One important thing is being able to face the most unpleasant tasks and doing them first. If you let them hang around for too long, they can just put you off your whole business. Sometimes the things that you're dreading doing aren't as bad when you actually do them. We've spent way more time worrying about doing them than actually doing them. As I've got more experienced in business, I've found it a bit easier to have the tough conversations, or to be a bit more ruthless when things aren't working. Just be quicker to call things that don't feel right. Trusting my instincts a bit more. Maybe in the first year or two I would have made some bad calls if I was too reliant on instincts. But now, I just get a feel if I've got somebody freelancing, taking a really long time, or overcharging on work, the ball's being dropped too much or I'm spotting mistakes that shouldn't be made, then I'll change things around a bit.

I've got a fixed list of questions and a way of doing the whole process of sourcing and launching products, and now when things feel a bit off, I'm much quicker to cancel them and do it a different way or find a new supplier or a new shipping company. For timekeeping I usually work just within school hours. I try not to work at night or at the weekends and I try and ride my horse or go skiing a few times a week, depending on the time of year. I really don't work even half time hours. I would say probably less than that. And that means when I am at my desk, I need to be super productive. I always finish each day with a list of what I need to do the next day. I have a free Google calendar that's shared with my team so they know when I've got a coaching call with a client, or with a group or if I'm traveling for a teaching weekend, or a trade show so I know where I am.

The rest of my family knows where I am and I don't get double booked. I use Calendly for booking any meetings with anybody external, which works really well. It's free, sort of links in with Google and that's worked really well just for making sure everything syncs up. When I have an email chat with somebody about having a call or a meeting and there's time zones, which there always are, then Calendly takes care of all that and pops it in my calendar for me. When I book flights or hotels, that always comes through and gets put in my calendar as well. It's been really good for managing time. There's the occasional slip-up, and I'm not the most organized person naturally, but that's generally 99% of the time between Calendly, a Google calendar and just sharing all projects on Skype and through Dropbox that has kept the show on the road.

During the last five years there's been some pretty big six and seven figure businesses all run through that same system. I work at the kitchen table. I've never had a separate office. I've never gone out the family home to work. The co-working spaces don't really work for me because I'm either recording training or doing coaching calls, so open plan offices don't work at all. The other thing that I quite like is just not having to commute. I can have a nice coffee at home, I can look at the southern Alps out my window and I can work on a rainy day. Then if the weather is good, I can go for a run or go riding or do something outdoors. I can plan my day around what needs doing and what else I want to do.

It's very flexible, which I love. If I occasionally need to do an evening shift or whatever, that's fine. But I've learned never to try and do calls with the children in the house. The more important the call, the rowdier they are and they just seem to know and it jinxes it. It's awful because then I end up hissing at the kids or sneaking around the house so they don't find me. It's not ideal. It's always really bad on every front if I try and juggle work and family all at the same time. I do try and keep that separation nice and clear. I don't have any fancy work tools or a desk. I've got a MacBook Pro, which is now pretty old, probably a couple of years old and I sit at an antique desk, which is one of my parents' old ones. It's actually out of a castle in Northumberland, so it's not some fancy office thing.

It just looks like part of the furniture and doesn't look like an office at all. I still haven't even bought an office chair, I just sit on a hard wooden kitchen chair! So that's been fine. I've never had any repetitive strain or aches or pains. I'm not sitting at my desk for a whole lot of time. If I'm talking to somebody on my team, I've got, say an hour long call with my assistant, then I'll often be going out after and go out for a walk by the lake and talk to her on a Skype call just on my phone, rather than sit at my desk and talk. I'd much rather keep moving and talk. I actually think better when I'm walking. I'm not productive if I haven't had fresh air and exercise. I always prioritize that as part of my weekly planning. And once a week on a Sunday, I plan the big things coming up for the week ahead.

If there's any travel, if there's any children logistics to juggle. I include things like children's play dates or sports days or things that I have to be at school, or want to be at school and then fit in work, things that I need to do in my own time. Then other work commitments that I've made for other people and then look at the week and it usually looks pretty good. Most of the time that works. Occasionally there's a spike, if I get sick or the kids are sick. Then there's travel and a backlog of people wanting coaching calls, that gets a bit ugly for a while, but that's not too often.

That's how I've managed to keep the balance. I don't find work nearly as stressful as I used to find my day job. I used to get terrible eczema when I worked in government. I used to come home just about bleeding on the inside of my elbows. I would just scratch myself raw and that was just pure stress. As soon as I did my own work, sure there's stressful moments when you've got your own business, but I've certainly had a much healthier lifestyle overall and really enjoy that. It's really nice. Even though I work from home, I seem to find that separation of working at home and just being at home quite easy and that's been working really well.

When it comes to your own productivity, everybody's wired a little bit differently. Some people love the feeling of ticking off a to do list. Some people are great starters, others procrastinate. Some love the feeling of finishing a project. Some people really like project managing things and being very organized, having big projects and structures and timelines. The thing that works best I think, is just that 12 week year for mapping out the big pieces that are important. The big chunky projects. And then each day, just making sure you don't get lost in things like social media. If you hang out in Facebook pages, thinking you're going to get useful answers to your most important business questions, you're probably not going to do too well because it's just full of lightweight fluff. It's a complete time vampire and it's not productively spent time. The best time you can spend is developing your own products or services that can keep selling without you, and then working on marketing to promote those.

Anything that you do as a one off that keeps being reused is the best use of your time and anything that's sort of administrative or repetitive, that's something you should be looking at outsourcing. The Richard Caution, Perry Marshall Book, 80/20 Sales and Marketing has got some great tips on how to do that really well. How to get really efficient in your business. Spending your time on the high value income earning stuff that only you can do and really outsourcing aggressively everything else or just not doing it. There's lots of things I just don't do or say no to because they don't really help the big picture. They might be nice to do. Maybe other people do them. Like social media for example. I don't do any social media, no Facebook, no Instagram, no Twitter, nothing. I haven't felt like I've missed out or that my business has been suffering because of it. I do paid Facebook ads, but I do no social media contacts. I shared nothing about my private life and I really like that that way.

That's how I manage my work/life balance and get through the big projects that I need to do. It's also useful to know whether you're a morning person or an evening person. I'm hopeless working at night, and usually have the children asleep in the house and it's just not a great time for me to work. I like to have dinner and then switch off. I do my hardest work in the morning. I never like doing coaching calls at night. I used to, in the early days, I used to have some UK clients who would dial in their morning, my New Zealand evening and I dreaded it all day. I never got to relax until that last call was over. I much prefer just front loading my day and then as soon as the children are home from school at three, that's it. I'm done. Most days of the week I'm done well before then.

It's important to be really proactive, to get the balance and to design your lifestyle. Then fit the work into the time you've got. I never want to be another "busy" person flat out and frazzled. If you're too busy, then maybe you need some help or should get better at saying no. If it means you've got to make a bit of a leap to get some help to be able to free yourself up to grow, that's a good investment. Just manage that growth carefully and go for staff who are quality and who've got a bit of breadth rather than somebody with a very narrow set of skills. I've hired some really great people that have taken on all sorts of additional responsibilities, beyond what I initially hired them for because they're just good all rounders. Sensible and good problem solvers. I trust their judgment. If they've got initiative and good judgment then they're capable of all sorts. There'll be real assets in your business.

You need to like them as well. Hire people to help you grow your business. You enjoy doing work with and spending time with because you'll be talking to them a lot, trusting them a lot and letting go of your business and letting go of control. There'll be other people coming in to help do your to do list. Make sure you've got clear to do lists and you hire the right people to help you get through it.

CHAPTER 6

WHAT MAKES A SUCCESSFUL ENTREPRENEUR

What makes a successful entrepreneur? How that helps you work towards clear future results and be really excited and motivated about how your life is going to change. But what makes a good entrepreneur?

Assuming you've done that work, you know what you want and why you want it. What are the things that separate who does well and who doesn't, as an entrepreneur? I've coached and worked alongside and been in groups along with lots of entrepreneurs over the last few years. I used to teach entrepreneurship and work in a university where my job was finding inventions in the university and commercializing them. I was working with the most inventive academics and then trying to find entrepreneurial students doing graduate programs in those subjects who were interested in jobs, developing those bits of technology to turn into real businesses or licensing opportunities.

As part of that, I used to teach the science faculty's entrepreneurship program. I've studied entrepreneurship at MIT. I've spent a lot of time looking at the theory of entrepreneurship, but over the last five or so years where I've been working on my own and running some of my own new ventures, and also working alongside other people I'm coaching, there's a real range in how people tackle each opportunity that's in front of them. On a course, everybody's got the same content, the same Facebook group, the same access to coaches, yet the results and the uptake are massively different. Terrifyingly, a very large number of people just don't do the work.

The number one thing to be a successful entrepreneur is to show up, learn the basics and to put things into practice. It's more than just sitting watching videos. It's taking action and implementing each step as you go. These don't need to be big steps. The smaller the steps you make, then the more likely you are to finish them and get onto the next one. That's really important.

The other factor is called a grit. This is something that a scientist called Carol Dweck has written about, and the book called Grit. If you need to know what makes people hardworking and driven and have that stickability and the ability just to grind out the work and hang in there, even when the going gets tough, Grit is a really good book to read.

I'd say that for success in business, grit is the one thing you can't go without. It's the one essential factor, because when the tough get going, the going gets tough. What we see is people that stop when there's a challenge or a stumbling block or delay, are never going to make it in business, but the people that find something else to learn while they're waiting, think creatively to get around it, pay for some professional help to get a faster answer to their problem, or think using their own brains, how they could solve this problem themselves. These are the people that smash through barriers and get ahead to the next level.

Another good book is called The Obstacle Is The Way. That's by Ryan Holiday, who's a top thinker, an original thinker and he has a stoic philosophy which is my own philosophy too. He believes in hard work and using your mind. Doing the work to get the result you want, as well as obviously having a great idea to work on.

In the coming chapters, we're going to start digging into the different business models that may suit you. To be a successful, true entrepreneur, which I would define as someone who creates something. They drive it themselves. They scale it. They might even think about selling it one day. They're really going for it as a business owner who's created something. There's definitely some element of creativity and there's definitely some element where they're the one who's come up with the idea and driven it.

There's definitely entrepreneurial people who can come and work for you, if you've had an idea that are great at being a productive and making these new ideas come to life. But, my definition of an entrepreneur for this chapter is somebody who can come up with the idea and make it happen.

If you're looking at something like a software business or an app, you're coming up with the idea. You're finding the skills, finding the funding if you need it, building the platform, testing it. You're getting initial customers, shipping a minimum viable product, getting feedback on that, improving it and you're making sales. That's the start of a real business. That's a business where potentially you're not selling your hours for dollars in that business. It's a platform. Maybe a software tool or something like that.

If you can create that, you need to have a certain amount of technical skill, and a lot of grit, drive, determination and a good work ethic. You're going to have to find time and energy to push into all those new areas that are going to be foreign at first and hard at first. If you're clear on the vision and you've got the grit, then you'll get there, whether you take five attempts or it ends up being product c, d or e. That's the one that's financially viable and that the market wants. But you just get in there, get started and do the work.

There's plenty of people who aren't quite that full blown entrepreneur. They don't want the risk. They don't want to remortgage, raise the money or put everything on the line for this business. There's a kind of hybrid model, which is running a business of your own, but it's not quite the same as the classic startup, where there's a startup team and a runway to get sales before you run out of funding.

A more moderate hybrid model would be e-Commerce, something like an Amazon business or a drop shipping business. You're creating a product of your own and building the store. You're building the listings, doing the research to find out what your customers are looking for and finding a point of difference with yours. It's not a copy and paste business model. It's definitely one with original thinking and reading the market, working with designers, working with developers, doing whatever needs to happen with your supply chains around the world to ship real products into the hands of real customers. The income can be quite passive on Amazon and is more high maintenance if you're running Facebook ads or handing your own shipping and customer service.

E-Commerce is a really nice model that's very scalable, if you're using Amazon to do your fulfillment. If you've got a supplier drop shipping your product, then you don't need all the warehousing and things as well. You need to be a little bit of a generalist to be able to get through all the things like working with designers, as well as running pay per click advertising, dealing with supply chains and barcodes, listings and links and all the other bits that go with a products business.

Quite a variety of tasks, but that's a scalable business. That can be a six or seven figure business that is part-time hours with no ongoing cash requirements beyond your startup costs. If you've got a budget of $5,000 you can start an Amazon business and it can scale. I started my Amazon business with a $300 initial investment, and that first product did over $1 million in sales in the first year. It was all bootstrapped. It was all grown through profit. No borrowing, no credit cards, no business partnerships, just really clean profit driven growth. That's a really nice model that I'm personally very fond of just because I've got the most experience in it and had great results in it.

But there's other models like that too. Being an agency owner is showing leadership. It's not quite the same as say a software startup company that's in Silicon Valley with all the pressure and hype that comes with that game. But it's definitely a responsibility. There's definitely great quality service required. You need to market yourself and have a point of difference. You need a compelling offer and to make a profit. You'll need a team. You'll need clients. You'll need processes and systems to deliver the service consistently.

Whether that's writing somebody's social media content, doing somebody's Amazon ads for them, doing somebody's YouTube videos for them, whatever it might be. Those agency models can be really nice because as soon as you've got a capable team under you and a way to generate leads, get the sales, the customers coming in and ordering and paying up front, then you get your team to deliver and you get to keep the profits.

With a decent sized team and a good offer, those can be quite big businesses. You've got some staff costs to cover, and depending on the nature of the service, those staff might be quite expensive. Artificial intelligence is quickly getting better logos than graphic designers could. Copywriting is always going to be done by humans for the foreseeable future, I would say. But keyword research needn't be or pay per click advertising as well. A lot of that's software driven now. But creating videos or anything like that, wherever there's a service, that tends to be reasonably high rate of pay, but your clients will pay even more.

There's always an opportunity there to offer a service to business owners. The more you understand those business owners, the better. If I was going to offer a service to a business, I would look at a service for Amazon business owners because I know that type of person really well. I know their type of business and all the things that go into it and the standards that are needed and the cost of competitive products. I just know that world, so it's easier for me to make a service offering to that market. Whereas if I tried to go and start doing graphics videos for YouTubers I'd be right on the back foot and I wouldn't have an advantage at all.

For you, if you're thinking about running a service business, try and make sure you get out of it being just you trading your hours for your dollars. Think of a way where you can get a bit of structure and some hierarchy where there might be some really low cost labor doing some of the grunt work. Somebody on commission may be getting sales or maybe you can automate the sales through some paid advertising that leads people through a sales funnel.
We'll talk about sales funnels later.

But customers sign up without needing a business development team is excellent. They place their order. Your team gets given their order and off they go and do the work. But if you are drumming up the business and delivering it all yourself, then it's very difficult to scale. You're still on the end of the phone when the client wants something. If they all come at once, you've got to do the work all at once and if it goes quiet for ages, nobody's paying you.

Although with a team you have a commitment for their salaries if they're employed. If they're just freelancing and just getting paid as they do each job behind the scenes and you've kind of got a virtual agency, that's a really nice model as well. We'll talk more about that. Some of the other models are things like being a person who works from home, so kind of freelancer. You could be a project manager or do somebody's admin, or work independently doing what you do for a high hourly rate. That could be just supporting somebody who's got another business, and you run your own business, but do five or 10 or 20 hours a week for somebody else. That gives you all the income you need. It's always nice to have more than one source of income.

If you don't have the leadership skills or the ambition or want the risk of carrying a whole team for an agency, you can still carve out a really nice lifestyle doing your own business, plus a little bit of work for somebody else as well, but from home and on your terms and using your skills and doing work that you enjoy.

The reason that people are successful is that they find a model that works for them. They do something that suits them. That they don't get bored of, that they don't find frustrating, that they stick in their lane. Know your strengths and know your personality. As we go through all the different business models in more detail, you'll quickly find out which models really suit you the best. You don't want to be forcing a square peg into a round hole.

If you're creative, don't give yourself a job where you're doing boring, repetitive work. If you're hopeless with technology, for goodness sake, don't end up trying to stitch apps and pixels and software tools together to run a multinational Shopify site with drop shipping and email database connectivity. Just make things easier for yourself and do what you're good at because there's always somebody who needs what you're good at. You can't do everything yourself.

The key to success is really just getting in the right lane and doing the work to to master your game. You'll need to do some learning and development to get some shortcuts to success. You'll need some grit to get through the work, and you'll need to be excited and motivated by a future state that will keep your motivation levels up as the going gets tough. That's all there is to it. There's no secret formula.

You don't need a fancy high powered coach. You don't need 40 hours a week free. Some of the most successful people have got the least amount of hours free. Again, you don't need a huge budget. I've seen some really successful entrepreneurs forced to be creative because they're on a tight budget. Then they came up with some much better solutions and ways of doing business than they would if they were a bit lazy or sloppy or just because they could throw more money at it to make the thing happen. Sometimes necessity forces brilliant work.

Everybody's got constraints and don't let constraints or excuses stop you doing what you're capable of. Whether it's budget or time, don't let either of those be an excuse for not aiming really high with your business. You can do whatever you want. You can do anything, but you can't do everything. Just make sure you put the time and effort in now to figure out the best track for you to financial freedom. An accountability partner can help you stay motivated and on track.

You'll be excited to see that the next chapter's now start going into more detail on the different business models. There's pros and cons to all of these. Some are more expensive, some of these have higher ongoing running costs. Some take longer to monetize and get a return on. Some of them take more time to write content or create videos. Others are quite good for generalists. Others are good for technical people. Some are great for creative.

We're going to go through a whole bunch of different business models. People that like working with people would love coaching or creating courses or running an online community. If you're more of a details and analytical kind of person then maybe some pay per click agency type of work, setting something up like that, or creating some software that solves a business problem. So many things out there you can do.

Let's get into the business models now and help you find the right track for you and make sure that as you start upskilling, learning and reading, you're following and being motivated by role models who've got the same sort of strengths as you. There's no point someone who's really introverted and shy wanting to be like Oprah Winfrey. If you can't think creatively or enjoy the creation stage of a project and new ideas, then Richard Branson is not a role model for you.

You want to find somebody who's like you, who's done well, see how they've done it and replicate that success. Following their tracks because successful people leave clues. There's plenty of opportunities out there and it's so wonderful seeing people get in their groove and find work that's fun and easy. It should be fun and easy. It shouldn't be a slog.

There will be stressful moments, but in general your own business should be a source of freedom, fun and learning, as well as income. What we want to do is help you get the rest of the skills you need and bundle it all together so you're up and away as fast as possible.

CHAPTER 7

BUSINESS MODELS

In this chapter, I want to start sharing with you some different business models. A good book if you haven't come across it is called, Business Model Generation. It doesn't matter whether you are selling a product or a service. There are some fundamental parts to your business that will need to be there for it to be a successful business. You need to have a product or service for sale that you can deliver. You need to have some kind of marketing to let potential customers know that it exists, which could be through paid advertising. It could be through PR. It could be through partnerships or affiliate partnerships, but some way to let people know about your product or service that you're selling.

And then when you find a customer who wants to buy your product, they need to be able to access all the information they need to know to make their purchase. That is possibly through a website, or it could be through just a simple landing page rather than a full website with very few distractions, just funneling them through to that 'Buy Now' button.

And then when they hit Buy Now, you need to have a way of processing their payment via credit card through PayPal or a Stripe transaction. We'll talk more about service providers later on who can help you automate this part of your business because it's really good if you're not mucking around with individuals taking payments over the phone or anything like that. You really want to get that automated completely, very secure and reassuring for the customer too knowing that their card is being processed securely.

As soon as the card has been charged or the payment gone through, you will usually then need to communicate to your customer that you've received their payment and the product or service will be on its way. If that's a physical product, you might then have tracking numbers and things to email out. You'll need some database to communicate with your customer.

For individual transactions, you might have some automatic email sequences that go out. You might also have some messages that go out through your database for marketing as well or just to announce new product launches, or seasonal offers, or just to keep your list of customers engaged and interested in what you do. When you have products to sell or they're looking for something to buy, they think of you.

Those are some of the fundamental building blocks of your business. You need a team that delivers all the operational side. My preference is always to automate as much of that as possible. I would much rather have a sales funnel with a video sales letter explaining what the service is all about, than me doing a phone call with somebody one on one saying exactly the same thing to explain what the service is all about.

It's really important from a legal point of view that when that is all done online that you've got things like a privacy policy, refund policy and disclaimers. There's a bit of detail to get right there. It's not hard. But it's important to get it right if you breach these then companies like Facebook won't let you sell a product or service. If there isn't a disclaimer and a privacy policy on the page that you're selling, your ads will be closed down.

The product or service is then delivered. That could be done in a range of ways. It might be you doing some consulting for someone. It could be shipping a product from Amazon. The mechanics will look very different depending on your product or service.

Then you need to have a way to maintain your relationship with the customer to make sure it's delivered consistently and to make sure that on the backend of your business, you're doing things like paying yourself, putting money aside for taxes, making sure anybody in your team who works for you is getting paid. That you're tracking your expenditure against your income so that you know how much profit your business is making. There's quite a few moving parts to get together.

Business Model Generation is a really great book to just look at those building blocks with lots of worked examples of different case studies of different types of business because all businesses have all of those core building blocks.

As we start to look at different business models within these online entrepreneurship opportunities, you will notice a few big categories. I want to run through these with you now. This is a fairly short summary, but when you see one that looks like it's the one that would most appeal to you, you can do is head over to freedomnavigator.com. You'll be able to sign up to my online program where you can learn exactly how to go about implementing each of these building blocks for all the different types of business model. There's more detail than we can go into in this book. This is to give you a high level idea of what's out there and which business model suits which profile entrepreneur.

If you're doing a high tech startup, you're raising capital, building software, going to go global and it's a really big opportunity, then your work ahead looks very different. The personality of the person who would lead that is very different to somebody who wants 20 hours a week freelancing from home doing a bit of copywriting or creating content for somebody else's social media pages.

The nice thing about these business models is the e-commerce platforms or social media platforms can come and go, these models remain the same and the certain skills and attributes of successful entrepreneurs who can run these different types of businesses.

ADVERTISING MODEL

I'm a really big fan of paid advertising because it's easy to measure the dollars going in. You can track this through the thank you page from the checkout page. When it goes through and says, "Thank you for making a purchase," you can track who's been through from Facebook, or a Google ad to the thank you page of your website. It shows that the customer saw the ad which cost you x dollars and then bought the product which made you yeah dollars. You can then work out what profit you made from that and what your return on investment for your advertising.

Advertising on different platforms requires slightly differ-ent skills. On Facebook, you need to have quite a broad range of skills to run really good advertising services for a client. Whether it's you doing it on your own or you running a team as an agency, both are absolutely fine. But amongst you and your team, you're going to have to have the following skills.

You're going to need somebody who is a really good ana-lyst. If you're in charge of this business, this is probably got to be you. Otherwise, you're going to be at the mercy of whether the analyst you hire are really doing their job well. You need to dive into the numbers, enjoy that detail, enjoy the fine tuning and optimizing. This really suits details people. If you are an automator or an analyst profile, then this is going to be a really good model for you.

It's not the only part. Analyzing the numbers and tweaking the campaigns to optimize the budget, to get the best return on investment for your client isn't the only thing. You also need to create offers so the advert itself needs to have some mes-sage and imagery that gets the customer excited enough to go ahead and click on it. Then go through to the offer and go ahead and purchase the offer.

In the advertising world, you also need to understand the point of difference of the product. You need to understand the psychology of the customer and need somebody really good at graphics so you can create eye-catching graphics. You need somebody who can commit to ongoing learning and develop-ment because this game probably more than any of the others changes very fast. If video ads are all the rage on Facebook one year, next year maybe everybody shifted over to Facebook messenger chats or retargeting. The way that pixels are done, the interface of all the different platforms always changes. I don't think I've ever been to Facebook ads and it's the same way twice. They're always tweaking it, changing the algorithm and changing what works.

Plus the other marketers out there who are running ads as well, they're figuring out things that work. When they're popular, they teach other people or do lots of it. Then the impact of that new eye-catching tactic that was working, slows down and stops working. If advertisers are exploiting loopholes or being a bit tricky, then Facebook, Google, YouTube or Amazon will close those loopholes down really fast to make sure that customers are seeing relevant adverts and not seeing any offensive adverts.

There's some terms of service that you've got to be aware of. On Facebook, you're not allowed to promote work from home schemes, cryptocurrencies schemes, adult products or diet products which is good for protecting consumers. But often, your clients might be in those fields. Then you've got a challenge getting creative messages out that are allowed by the advertising platform but still lead to great sales for your client.

I think advertising knowledge is a wonderful skill to develop because all products and services need some form of promotion. It's great that you can measure the return on investment so accurately. So, advertising is the first model. And it suits people who are analytical. It also suits generalists. You need to be able to sell and be comfortable pitching your service to the client. This isn't something where somebody is going to hire you without a conversation and you demonstrating and understanding their product and service.

It's not all about the numbers. It's definitely a skill that's got a mix of marketing and data analysis and optimizing those offers. You're going to have to work with the client in an ongoing basis. They'll have different campaigns, new products, new offers coming out all the time. Your job will be to create videos, or images, the text and load them all up. Run those ads, measure the results, improve the results and report back showing the results from your work.

Advertising is a great model. It can be done from anywhere in the world. A lot of the creative and graphic skills are very cheap. My favorite tool for creating Facebook ads is Canva. There's also various very talented people on platforms like Fiverr who can do animated videos. You might need to commission somebody to create videos. You might be working with photographers or people doing video shoots or capturing your client doing voice to camera videos. Then you're using those as the creative for your ad campaign.

As an advertiser, there'll always be new things to promote and campaigns to measure and tweak. It's stimulating, using high brain power and is quite challenging. It's not just a one-dimensional simple repetitive task. You've really got to have your brain working and get to be great at advertising. You've got to really stay current with what's working.

AFFILIATE MARKETING

The second model is affiliate marketing. This is a really neat model too because you don't need to own anything. Your job is being a promoter. This is where I've seen people have $10 million days as an affiliate for some of the big internet marketing courses. One of the first Amazon courses I ever did, I saw somebody make $10 million in a day on the day that the launched closed, because they built a huge following. They had people engaged and listening to them, committed to doing that program when doors closed.

And so when the doors closed, those customers were using a unique link that the affiliate marketer had created unique to them, that was issued by the people who owned the course or the program. Affiliate marketers build their own database. They educate them and make people aware of opportunities. They create offers and they might get exclusive offers. When the sale goes through, they get paid some form of commission. If they're an Amazon affiliate, they might get a very small percentage of sales. Or they might be somebody, say a mommy blogger promoting baby products in an article. There's a unique link there that Amazon recognizes as from that blogger. Any sales that are made from that link from that blogger of that product, Amazon will then give the blogger a small percentage commission.

On some of the internet marketing courses, the commission can be 50%. So it's a really great model. People do all sorts of clever stuff. They'll build their own database and they'll trade with somebody else's database. They'll cross-promote each other's office. If they're nice complementary offers, affiliate marketer one might be able to promote an offer to a different affiliate marketer's database. Then they'll switch back and do it the other way as well.

If the product is a high price, say a $5,000 course, then commission starts to get really substantial. You see affiliate marketers giving away iPads and all sorts of really generous benefits, or separate mastermind membership, or free coaching course. You'll see them go to great lengths to get those sales across the line using their unique links. It's great for people who create courses or programs because they don't need to do all the work themselves promoting. They'll go out to all the top affiliates who've got huge databases of people looking for work from home opportunities. The affiliate marketer will go out and tell their database all about this opportunity, this course, why it's so good, why they should do it. Then as the doors close or maybe on an ongoing basis, those sales will lead to really good commissions through to the affiliate marketer.

Now one caveat is that if a lot of people then refund, the affiliate marketer then doesn't get their commission. So it's usually a 30-day or sometimes a seven-day refund period. That means that the affiliate marketer's not incentivized to oversell it. They're not going to make up fibs to get people to buy, saying it's better than it really is because if people are disappointed and refund, they don't get paid.

It's a great model for people that like building a following, that like sharing opportunities and educating people. Some of the best affiliate marketers I've seen are people like Jason Fladlien and Dave Kettner, promoting the amazing selling machine. There's plenty of other people out there too.

Some of the courses I've seen that have got really good affiliate offers are the Wholesale Formula. They've got a series of webinars or videos that people who want to promote that program can share with their audiences. Then the affiliates and the company that owns the course go 50/50 on those payments, so great for everyone.

The nice thing is, you don't need to own or create anything. It really suits people that are good marketers and good at building a following. Usually these people are good copywriters. Maybe they're quite charismatic. They might have a YouTube channel and be diligent at writing regular emails. They're creating content that builds a following so that when there's an offer to make, they've got an engaged group who are ready to hit 'buy' and who trusts the affiliate marketer.

Some of them get quite aggressive! I'm on a few people's distribution lists. And I go, "Oh they must be building it for a launch because they suddenly go into overdrive." Then others I just learn a lot from and may or may not buy anything from them. They are building a database to promote other people's products, then they get a commission on the sales.

It's always good to have more than one source of income. If you're looking to do affiliate deals and you've got a product or service and a big database, you can always look for complementary products or services and approach people to do an affiliate deal. That's either you would sell somebody else's product or service to your database, or the other way around. You would find other people with a big database that might be interested in your product or service.

It can be pretty fun being an affiliate marketer. If you enjoy learning, you'll see what's working, the trends around different business opportunities or lucrative skills people are paying to learn. You can do this from anywhere in the world. You can have cheap labor working under you creating articles or polishing up the YouTube videos that you've done a raw cut. They can make it all much more professional, intros, jingles and things that will help you get more sales.

These people are sharing opportunities. They're great communicators and good at selling. They're good at marketing. People want to follow them, so that's a very personable person usually. You've got to have a lot of energy and drive those offers and opportunities. There's often a lot of work between the big promotions just to keep everybody engaged, following you and building that following.

It's a little bit different from being an influencer. That can involve affiliate type partnerships. But it's more likely to be paid per post or some kind of profit share on a single offer or some kind of giveaway, where the influencer is just paid a flat fee.

I'm not actually going to teach how to become an influencer in this book. I'll mention it briefly. My full course, we go into it in a little bit more detail exactly how it works, who it suits, how to do it and how to become an influencer and also how to use influencers.

Affiliate marketing is one of those big categories. It's a really neat online business model for people who are entrepreneurial, who want to work from home and are looking to create a profitable online business.

E-COMMERCE

The third model is e-commerce. This is one I'm particularly fond of. I have a bit of a soft spot for e-com for selling products through Amazon, Shopify website or your own website of any kind. Shopify seems to be a very popular one for products because the templates are so nice and easy to use and they convert so well. The trick with e-commerce is to find a unique product that is marketable. It must have a point of difference and the sale price is significantly higher than the price you pay for it. It sounds easy, but there's a lot to it. You've got to catch customers attention usually through either advertising on Facebook. It might be just getting your product ranked on Amazon, so it's visible and customers when searching for it on Amazon. So that's for getting traffic, that's the eyeballs that land on your product for sale. whether it's through Amazon, your own website, Ebay or Etsy.

Selling products is really cool because you're selling something tangible, real people who need real things. They can be recession proof or they can be luxury items. They can be pretty much anything. They can be $10 bottles of essential oil right through to furniture or tiny houses. E-commerce is really neat because you're selling stuff that people need and want. You can show a photograph of it and in turn makes the customer happy. It's something that they get real benefit from.

The component parts to being a successful e-commerce seller are having a bit of an eye for products. You can be the most analytical person in the world, but you still need to think of a point of difference for your product. You need to think how to brief the design and to come up with some nice looking packaging. You need a photographer to get some great shots and you need to write good copy. The important thing is you need to have a point of difference with your product.

You need to have researched the market, researched the competition, read the competitor's reviews and found your gap. Then you execute really well. You've got to keep your costs down, be very efficient with your shipping and negotiate well with the suppliers. The suppliers can be all around the world, there's quite a few moving parts.

If you choose the right product and get it ranked, it comes up on Google searches, on the top of Amazon pages, goes viral on Facebook, then you can have great ongoing sales. I've had products that I've launched on Amazon over five years ago that still make tens of thousands of profits every single month. I don't need to do anything else apart from stay in stock.

So e-commerce is a wonderful business model. It suits generalists and is very appealing to people who are creative. You're actually creating a real physical product of your own and creating a brand of your own which is very exciting. It's the most affordable way to create your own business where you actually own something physical.

The nice thing is that there are lots of well-established platforms that you can put your products on. You might need to pay for some advertising, but you don't need to build everything from scratch. No coding, no website. You can launch on Amazon or you can plug and play some Shopify templates. Set a Facebook brand page, run some ads from there, drive traffic to your listings and get the sale online. Then have your supplier do all the shipping and handling.

One reason I like using Amazon is because of Fulfillment By Amazon, or FBA. FBA means you don't need to handle the products yourself. There's no shipping the products yourself, dealing with tracking numbers, talking to customers, going down to the post shop. Amazon automates all that shipping and handling and customer service for you for just $40 something a month, which is a huge opportunity.

For most people who come to me saying they want to start an online business, I do believe Amazon is one of the best models out there because you can start with relatively low capital. It's not too time intensive. The upside when you choose the right products and build a brand, you can be up to a six or seven figure business potentially within a couple years. You can then sell an Amazon business that is low tech to run.

But the things you need to get right there is real grit. Amazon's a big platform, it's not intuitive and their rules change. There's policies that you've got to understand and there is advertising to run on the platform. You can spend your whole time just specializing on Amazon. It would keep you absolutely busy enough. You could just launch a dozen or a couple of dozen products. The right mix of products in that portfolio could lead to a six or seven figure income potentially, if you got the right mix. The people I see struggling with Amazon are very tightly controlled people who need perfect data and can't read trends or see an opportunity. Purely analytical people can struggle with the creative side of building a brand of physical products, Though there are a lot of exceptions to this rule too of course!

It's an appealing lifestyle. It can be done anywhere in the world like all of these models, but also a great income earner because most of that income is passive, once you've done the work at the front end to choose the product and set it up and get it ranked.

I'm a big fan of physical products for that reason. The buyer intent on Amazon is high. There's other platforms like Ebay, Etsy or even Google Shopping, or you can drop ship too. Drop shipping is a variation where instead of you buying the product and your own brand, stocking it somewhere and then it ships from the customer orders. With drop shipping, the customer places an order, then you let the supplier know that they need to ship one unit to that customer's address, then that all happens. It can be automated to some extent. There's apps that connect your supplier and their tracking numbers to your customer and your website. There's a bit of wiring together and it's much higher tech than Amazon, plus you've got to run adverts.

Amazon charges fees as a referral fee and the fulfillment fee when you make a sale. The nice thing is you don't need to pay a lot to get the customers to find your product. They are on Amazon looking for the product and they trust Amazon will sell them a good quality one and ship it on time.

With drop shipping or selling through your own website, you've got to get the customer to your site, build trust with them, get them to put that product in the cart, get them to give you their credit card details, check out and then give you their address. Then you've got to communicate with them yourself with the tracking details and follow ups.

My preference is for Amazon just based on my own experience. But, if you are slightly more technically minded and enjoy the analytical side of running ads, or you don't like the upfront cost of Amazon such as buying your private label product first to sell it on for a higher price second. The cash flow is a little bit easier with drop shipping or with wholesaling, which is why you buy in bulk from a supplier where you don't make it your own brand or product. You just sell a generic product on Amazon for a profit or on your own website.

E-commerce is a really neat model. There's people from all sorts of different backgrounds doing really well on e-commerce. I think that it suits generalists and creative people. It suits big picture people. You need to have a lot of grit and you need to be able to knuckle down and dig into the details when you need.

If you're running an Amazon pay-per-click campaign or setting up barcodes or instructing suppliers about shipping instructions, that stuff has to be done right. There's not a lot of room for error and there's a bit more money at stake. You're buying the product upfront. It's not just you selling your time. You're actually purchasing a product to resell.

That means if you're doing Amazon, you need to take it pretty seriously. Do the training. Don't make any rookie mistakes and make the most of this huge e-commerce opportunity because the platforms are just massive and growing. It double-edged rights. They're a real threat to high streets and malls where they just can't keep up with the range and the prices that companies like Amazon or Ebay or Etsy can offer online.

Etsy is a great platform for handmade, photogenic, beautiful products with a real feel good factor. You could have personalized products that are drop shipped. Or you could have handmade products from all around the world. It really suits creators or makers who want to actually hand-make their own products.

So that's another business model, making your own physical products and selling those. That could be through a farmer's market. That's pretty hard to scale compared to the ability to build it up through a website such as Etsy and sell your handmade products say jewelry through a platform like that.

E-commerce is wonderful, but it's not for everyone. You've got to project manage quite a few moving parts to make it all work. When you get it right, it can be extremely lucrative, very rewarding. For those creators who like seeing real things come to life, it's a very rewarding exercise to create and build your own brand. I've really enjoyed e-commerce. And that's probably the area I've had some of the best results in my business life. When we came upon the next one, courses and coaching, you'll see that that's another business model that's really appealing as well.

COURSES AND COACHING

This is a great way to share your specialist knowledge and it can be very lucrative. People often think they don't know much about anything. But based on your interests, or some life experience you've had, or through a job you've had in the past, or anything that you've invested in learning about yourself, often other people need to know that. It could be around parenting, riding your horse in dressage competitions, business coaching, how to do your own bookkeeping or how to use graphic design programs. It could be how to present on stage. So all sorts of different areas of life could be turned into online courses.

The more businesslike the course, the more your customers are willing to invest in learning it, because they can see they're going to get a return on investment. If I took a course on how to be a better speaker at seminars, that would have a real impact on my business's bottom line. My number of invitations to speak at conferences or give seminars would increase. Whereas a course on flower arranging might be really high on the feel good factor, but it's only really for personal interest. I wouldn't value that nearly as highly. Productivity or getting organised always appeal to people as courses to buy as well.

There's also a lot of free content out there. If you look at You-Tube, there's all sorts of people sharing how to do stuff you need to learn about. When you create a course, you want to build a community. You want to really stretch on how to get people through the program rather than just get lost and overwhelmed on a massive platform like YouTube. You can go around in circles and find contradicting advice. You want to make it really clear that when people join your program, they'll be led through start to finish with structure. They'll find everything they need in one place and get all the support they need. They need to feel reassured by that clarity and sense of community.

People want clarity and when they're stumbling around looking at free resources on their own, they're comparing it with free. But their time is precious. They're wasting a lot of time going around in circles or getting advice from the wrong people, or not sure if the advice is even correct. So people want certainty and clarity. That's what you want to provide with any online course you do.

There are some really cool platforms to host courses like Kajabi and Thinkific. They're really good for loading up your online videos. Then customers who bought the program can work their way through those. There can be downloads and it will have a checklist at the end of each section to mark that section is complete. Then they can move on to the next video. It's very easy to make it user friendly and easy for them to become a master in a subject that they're looking to learn about.

Whether it's how to run YouTube, how to do SEO, or how to create Facebook video ads, you can create courses that people will want. Generally the way that these courses are marketed is through a sales funnel. There maybe a Facebook ad or a YouTube ad catching people's attention with a problem or an opportunity that's going to interest them. Then they'll click and go to a page where they'll learn more about you, or your course, or what you can help them with. Then there's maybe a free download. Maybe the first chapter of a book is free. Or maybe there's a free webinar to watch where they get to know, like and trust you.

And then at the end of that, there's an offer. For $997, for example, you can then watch an eight-module course and become an expert in that subject. You're going to not make a lot of mistakes by doing this course. You're going to learn how to do it the right way by doing this course. You're going to save a lot of time by doing this course. You're going to get better results by doing this course. You're going to be less stressed because you're doing a course on the subject.

So if you want to look at a good example of this, there's a really good book by Jeff Hunt called The Website Investor. This is a short book that leads to a website, ironically a website about buying websites. On that website page, you'll learn exactly what's included in his fully comprehensive course of all the things you need to know if you're considering investing in websites. There's all the numbers to run, the questions to ask, the process, where to look, how to use brokers, how to use professional service people. It will step you right through all of that and give you a peace of mind.

If you're about to invest in a website, spending $1000 on a course and a few hours reading a book, and a few hours doing the course, this will be time well spent. You'll get a better result. You'll have more clarity, more peace of mind and you'll be less stressed by not knowing what you don't know.

Creating courses is great. I think that's preferable to coaching. One on one coaching is lucrative if you've got a very specialist area, but it doesn't really scale. You'll very quickly find your calendar where it's just like it used to be at day job, you're fully booked. People want you and there's messages between the calls. A lot of your energy goes into supporting other individuals.

Another nice way to do it is group coaching. If you want to learn from somebody who's been really successful at building the coaching model, Taki Moore has done a really great job. He's got a book called Million Dollar Coach. He teaches people how to do a leveraged version of coaching. A group model is a nice hybrid of income and scalability, while keeping your sanity and lifestyle. There is also some one on one time. There's a high end offer where people get to invest more and be part of a boardroom inner circle mastermind format and have more access to Taki or his other head coaches.

Very quickly in order to scale there needs to be a system that's not just you and your individual expertise. You need programs with strict checklists, almost a curriculum to the coaching and a best practice way of tackling that subject area.

Courses and coaching are very complementary. They suit people who are good with people. They suit people who enjoy teaching and who are happy presenting. It's not necessarily a bad one for introverts because you can do it all from home. It's not like you need to talk all day. But I personally found coaching quite draining if I did too much of it. Whereas a short burst, giving a presentation, or doing my live weekly webinar that I do every Friday morning, I find that really fun and it keeps me sharp. Whenever I do any surveys for the members of all my programs, the live Friday teaching session I do is always the most popular thing in my entire program because people can tell I'm in my element and I really enjoy that live teaching.

I used to teach entrepreneurship in a university, so that's just a format that I find easy and fun and I also get a lot out of it. My students get the benefit of being kept up to date and having a chance to ask questions.

Now there are other places to sell your course rather than selling it yourself through a Facebook ad through to a sales funnel. You can put your course up on Udemy. But when you see the price that Udemy charges for a course versus the value that's in the course, I wouldn't want to give away my hard-earned expertise at that price. I want to package it up and make it a much higher end experience for a smaller number of people.

You've got to watch a few things, like people downloading and copying the content or downloading it all within the refund period, and then just getting a refund. There's a few annoying things like that to contend with, but there's ways around that. We can do watermarks and stop downloads. That's not been a major problem, but just a few little extra things to be aware of.

Courses and coaching suit people who enjoy learning because people who like learning generally like teaching. They value it. It suits people that enjoy interaction with other humans. Some people are very happy to sit behind spreadsheets all day everyday. But I like to have a few quality conversations and quality interaction. It's not just doing something really repetitive or low level. There's something about teaching a subject that keeps you really engaged at your best in that area.

I found courses and coaching really neat. I've bought so many myself over the years I've seen what works in terms of format, style and delivery. I've had courses that are around Amazon that are eight modules, plus a few bonus modules and a bunch of downloads and resources. The price point for that can be between $1000 and even $5000. If you get above a couple of thousand dollars sale prices, generally the customers will want to have a conversation with somebody. You would set up a one-on-one call with you or somebody in a sales team. That person in your team can be on commission. You don't necessarily need to pay them an hourly rate.

But if you want to sell a course, you can either do it fully automated like the website investors $997. If you've read the book, you'll be pretty convinced that this is the man to learn from. The investment to do the full course is a really easy decision if you're serious about buying a website. Whereas a course costing $5,000, on how to become an accredited business coach or to do an NLP course, generally you would have a conversation with somebody from the organization who answers any questions and checks you're the right fit. They check you out. You check them out. Then the customer only goes ahead if that conversation's gone well. The person doing the sales calls has all the answers and gives them the reassurance to go ahead and invest.

So courses and coaching are great because you're trading some of your time but in a very lucrative way. The more you get into group coaching or online courses, the more leveraged your time and the more profitable it becomes and the more free time you've got. But sometimes just to earn the right to have the bigger programs, you might start with some one-on-one clients just to generate some extra cash flow. It's always nice to have more than one source of income because that means you don't have lots of pressure on one business that might be in high growth mode. You can keep reinvesting in that without having to suck money out of it to live off.

DIVERSIFY INCOME STREAMS

Two sources of income doesn't just double your income. It halves the risk. It makes you sleep better at night and it keeps things nicely diversified. You don't ever want to have all your eggs in one basket. Especially if your business is built on one of these big platforms like YouTube, Google or Amazon where Facebook can change the algorithm over night and people's businesses totally get a shake up way beyond their control. Their policy is completely beyond your control.

Google over the years has done a few really big algorithm changes. All the guys doing SEO to get products and services ranked for their clients at the top of page one, just disappeared off the face of the earth. That was really tough for them. Amazon changes the rules a lot too. Facebook changes the algorithms to make people pay for things that were free or to hide things that aren't paid. It's getting more and more commercial. Instagram advertising I'd include in there with Facebook advertising. It's the same company, just a slightly different format.

When you're using those big platforms, it is really nice to have a separate income stream through, something like coaching or running an online course. I employ a lot of people as coaches to help my new students who are veterans of my own coaching program. The people that came through that really impressed me and who got good results, who've got six and seven Amazon businesses of their own now; they're often really keen to do a few hours a week coaching for a good hourly rate that I pay them to help my new students.

When my new students sign up for an Amazon course, they get six one-on-one coaching sessions with a coach I've hand-picked which is a great offer for the student. It's an expense for me to deliver, but it means people get better results and get some one-on-one help with their product selection.

FREELANCING

One other model to look is freelancing. This is one that's appealing in some ways because Freelancing is great because you can use your skills, to do something that you're a master of. Whether it's writing copy for marketing purposes, doing graphic design because you're a designer or running pay-per-click advertising for a client. It might be something like editing photographs or Photoshopping images for Amazon sellers. It can be sold through gigs. If you've heard about the gig economy, these are platforms like Fiverr where people can advertise a service. They charge $5 and upwards for that service. The platform Fiverr takes a commission when somebody orders their service. People are looking on that platform when they need some work done. That's where they go to find a copywriter, or an editor, or a graphic designer, or someone to do a logo, someone to help edit some emails for marketing or to help them develop a website.

Upwork, Fiverr, Freelancer, and a bunch of others are really great websites for freelancers to post their skills and find paid work. It doesn't always scale very well. But you can be quite efficient. You can have another team beneath you. So you might win the work and then outsource it behind the scenes to somebody at a lower cost. Maybe something like removing the background to an Amazon image to make it white or transparent is a three-minute job for you, but you get paid quite a lot to do it. So it's not huge money, but it's also a tiny amount of time.

So some of those freelancing jobs could be really fun. If you are responsive but flexible, you can fit in with clients getting their work turned around quickly. But you're doing work in and around your other business or other day job. So freelancing is a great way to start getting that feeling of your own money, your own business. You don't need to go out and create a whole website or do anything really fancy. You can offer your time and your skills to help other people who need those services. And you can just do what you're good at and get paid a good hourly rate for it. The better the testimonials and level of experience you've got and the good reviews showing on those platforms like Fiverr or Upwork, the more you're going to get booked and the more you can put your rate up.

I found all of my virtual assistants, graphics people, editors, everyone I've used for all parts of my business I find online through those platforms. Rarely you'll find someone who doesn't deliver, generally they're pretty good. They want the work and they'll do a great job. It doesn't cost the earth so it's a great service to use. If you want to offer a service, you could move your price up as your skills, experience and reviews go up. It could be a nice little side income stream.

Some of the better paid freelancing skills are things like designing sales funnels. That can be a really nice one. If you become proficient at click funnels or designing Shopify pages that convert, all those things that help other business owners get more sales or get more customers to the door. Those are the premium skills to work on those, the ones that people really value highly. Whereas something like doing some basic customer service, there's a lot of cheap alternatives for you to do those things. Try and focus on high end offers.

You can also always work on a commission, like freelancing for somebody who's got a program and you do their sales calls. They might have a $5,000 course. You do the sales calls or the discovery calls, to check out whether they're a good fit for the course. If you have a good conversation and they go ahead and buy, then you might get 10% or 20% commission on that sale. It's not really true freelancing, but it's just a thing where you could set up your calendar each week to be available to do five or ten calls. Some of those will lead to a nice commission payment.

We've been through quite a few of the different business models. There's a lot more on social media. Creating content for social media posts or becoming an influencer, which we won't focus on too much now. It's pretty much always going to fall into advert freelancing category or some kind of affiliate marketing. Usually if you're creating content for someone else, it's kind of a freelancing marketing job. You're writing posts for them, or you're doctoring images and editing graphics and things to make their posts look good. Maybe you're working on offers with other people for them.

There are lots of different business models out there. But they generally fall into those broad categories around advertising, affiliate marketing, e-commerce, courses and coaching, or freelancing. When you did the profiling quiz, you will have had a report that gives you some suggestions based on your profile, which models would work best for you.

I hope that's been useful, understanding a bit more about what else is out there. What business model suits you, which kind of people, because not all people will find all these business models as easy as unless you're very technically minded. You'll be quite happy stitching bits of software and apps together and getting databases to talk to websites, to talk to payment pages, and track pixels. That's just up your alley. Whereas other people who can talk to clients all day, help them with their problems and their questions and get a lot of energy and good feedback from that kind of work. So pick the model that suits you best.

In the full program, the Freedom Navigator Course, we'll be going through exactly how to set these up. We'll be looking at case studies for each, best practice for each, exactly step by step how to go about becoming each of these types of online entrepreneurs.

You want to make sure you pick the one that's right for you. If you go down the wrong track and you're really forcing yourself into a model that doesn't suit you, then you're going to find it hard work. If you choose something that comes naturally to you, the results will be better. You will have a lot more fun and it will flow. You'll take off and just streak ahead. Make sure you pick the right model for you. That's what this program and the profiling quiz is all about, making sure you're aware of what's out there and picking a model that really suits you.

One model I haven't covered here is multilevel marketing, MLM. I'm not a big fan of that because it's not really online, nor quick to monetise usually. While I've seen a lot of people get very enthusiastic, there are lots more who get no results or go backwards. It takes a very long time to build up those recurring payments, it's not passive and comes at a real social cost when you pump your networks to buy the products. The people that have made it to the top are very vocal and it gets a little bit skewed. Everybody thinks it's wonderful because they hear some single figures of amazing case studies. Generally for most people, I think that's a slow burn to be an income stream that you can live off.

Whereas all these other ones, I'd like to think that within six to 12 months, they could be your main source of income if you do everything following best practice. Obviously individual results can vary, but these are all models that are capable of that level of take off and give you the lifestyle that you want.

CHAPTER 8

SELLING BUSINESS

I was about 18 months into selling products on my first e-commerce store. I have a friend who's a business broker in the states, he's an Australian guy and he specializes in selling websites. I'd just finished my tax year end, all my paperwork and accounts were all neat and tidy. Everything was accounted for and squared up and I could see how much profit my last financial year had been. So I contacted Jock and asked him what he thought my business might be worth because I thought maybe in a few years if I sold it, it'd be quite nice to. From that point on we would start preparing it the right way and getting everything set up so it could be sold one day. Much to my surprise, Jock came back and reckoned it was worth $1 million right now, US, and I said, "Well, if you get me that, I would take it."

The next day, Jock had found me a buyer from his list who asked a lot of questions. He sent some professional services, lawyers and accountants through to ask even more questions. And they were happy with the answers and they went ahead. This guy who was a private investor in Utah, bought my first business that I'd started.

It was only 18 months old. I'd only recently given up the day job, but I'd started a second Amazon brand that was growing fast as well and I thought some extra cash to tip into that would be nice. Plus, it would be the end of our mortgage. It meant we could maybe go and do something that we otherwise wouldn't be able to do, like my husband would give up his job and we'd go off to Bali for three months. So we did that before our eldest son started school.

We got to do some really cool experiences and clear a serious amount of debt. Which then totally changed what we needed to earn each month because we didn't have a mortgage anymore. We moved down south to the South Island of New Zealand. We had been in the capital city and now we live in the middle of nowhere, in the mountains, amongst the ski fields with a horse and a totally different lifestyle, thanks to selling the business.

These big, one off paydays can really change the game. They are ideally lumps of cash, rather than some sort of payment based on performance over a few years. Otherwise, really why bother? You'd be taking that profit out of the business at that rate anyway. So, it's always good to get cash upfront and then you've got some purchasing power for whatever you want to start next. You've got some ability to quickly clear some debt and avoid paying all those pesky banks all that interest over the length of a mortgage, or any other debt that you want to clear.

That was a really liberating move, getting rid of the mortgage and moving to where we really wanted to, our dream location. We don't have a really lavish lifestyle. We do things that mostly are the hobbies of millionaires. There's skiing and horses and they're not cheap hobbies, but they don't cost a lot because we live where they happen. We live amongst the ski fields, so we have a season pass. The children go skiing every Thursday for school, so we're up there at least one day a week for that. Then there's the local kids program all day Sunday, so two days a week skiing minimum in the winter.

I've got a horse and we go out on the lake, the quality of life is wonderful, but it doesn't all cost a lot of cash. It's not like the cost of going on a ski holiday when you live in a city somewhere else and you're paying for a chalet and eating out every meal or renting gear or all the short passes rather than a whole season pass. Getting rental cars, all that stuff that becomes really expensive if it's not at your doorstep.

I've really designed the lifestyle and moved to the place I want. The children are in a fantastic school, which is the local school and is free. It's one of the best schools in the country, it's just amazing the stuff these children get to do, so they're having a wonderful childhood. I've got fast Internet speed, that's my lifeblood, and live in a warm house in a beautiful town in the mountains.

Life is really great and there's definitely always ups and downs as a business owner, you can be sure, that's guaranteed. There's going to be tough bits to figure out and work through. Other times where you get some great results and it makes it all worth it.

Over the last five years, I've now sold two businesses and I'm planning on selling another one again soon. I think products businesses are very appealing because they can be sold without it really relying on the founder to run it. It's not like it's my reputation behind those products that sell on a website or on Amazon, it's the products that sell. I've just chosen them, branded them and got them up and ranked and selling. Those are very easy businesses to sell.

A coaching business is much harder to sell and something like affiliate marketing could be sold, but the person buying it's going to have to commit to quite a lot of ongoing work. Advertising those agencies, the best way to exit those is probably to sell out to another agency. If you've got an Amazon advertising agency, you could sell out to somebody who does YouTube or Facebook ads and do a merger and acquisition model. Rather than just sell your cash flow to some independent investor who just wants a business to own. It's more likely you'd merge into someone else in the industry as a strategic acquisition rather than just an asset sale.

We're very lucky in New Zealand in that any assets that we sell don't get any capital gains tax. That's been helpful as well. Some of those other businesses that we've talked about in the book, things like freelancing, they're almost impossible to sell. So that's why those product and service businesses, where it's not all about you delivering it, that's why they're so neat. Always think about that, if you think you might want to sell your business one day.

From the beginning, be prepared to let go, make sure you hire staff who are competent and can run the thing without you having to watch over them every minute, hold their hands and pat them on the back to keep them going. You want independent people working hard, being well rewarded for doing good work, but it doesn't all come down to you pushing everything along, every day to make things happen. It's going to be really hard for you to have a holiday or sell the business if it all comes down to you all the time.

It's good discipline to pretend you're selling your business because then all your systems are in order, you focus on profit because that's how the valuation will be reached, based on a multiple of your profit. It'll let you have neat systems and standard operating procedures and everything documented. When it comes to your year end, all your accounts will be nice and neat and you'll have filed all your invoices in the right place, there's no big shoe box of receipts three years later.

Selling your business makes you run your business better and you think about, "How will people pick holes in my strategy? How will I sign up the supplier and make them sign this confidentiality agreement?" Or that it would be a virtual assistant who signs up their contract, would transfer to a new owner. All those things are really important. Just as a principal from the beginning, just build it as if you're going to sell it.

There's a really good book by John Warrillow called Built to Sell, which goes through all the different ways to build and sell your business, that's really good. It makes a huge difference to the track your life's on, if you can collect a big lump sum. I've done it a couple of times and I'm certainly looking forward very much to doing it again.

For whatever reason you start your business, at some stage you'll either wind it up or exit, or partner with someone or sell it. It's good to think about that from the beginning because when the market changes, you want to be ready for that, and not left behind. You want to get out when your valuation is the highest, if you think you're going to sell. You want to time it when the market's good as well, not just the business itself is going well, but when the market's is looking to buy and your story's attractive.

Even seasonal stuff. If you try and sell something to an

e-commerce person in quarter four, good luck. There'll be absolutely flat out just trying to stay in stock and ride that spike that comes at the end of each year in quarter four. But in quarter one or two, they'll be all cashed up. Chinese New Year's happening and they'll be looking for new products to launch, and that's a great time to sell. Maybe the end of the financial year is a good time to do a transition, when everything ends with one year end and the start of the next one goes to the new owner.

Think about timing, there's a few considerations there. We'll go into that more in the course. If you are thinking that you might be ready to start your business and you want to find out more about all these different business models, advertising, affiliate marketing, e-commerce, freelancing, generating content or having a course or coaching business, then head over to freedomnavigator.com. There you can enroll and do a fully comprehensive training that really steps you through all the things you need to know to start your own business. Depending on what profile you are, what business model appeals to you the most. You might even do a couple of things, but you'll have everything there you need to get started. We'll give you some really good references and resources so you can get off on the right track and start your own business the right way and choose the business that really suits you.

CHAPTER 9

FREEDOM NAVIGATOR

Everybody's capable of running their own business, even alongside a day job. When I started mine, it's one of the best things I did. Helping other people is incredibly rewarding and it's been amazing to see other people get really good results from businesses that they've started or businesses I've helped them with. Even people that I've employed, there's been some really amazing people that have come and worked for me over the years and it's been really nice being able to give them interesting work and learning and travel opportunities. I've really enjoyed working with my small teams.

If you're thinking about doing this, starting an online business, then I can strongly recommend that you just do it and give it a try. It gives you all sorts of unexpected nice feelings, being a business owner. There's a nice thing seeing that extra stream of income coming through, but it's also nice to be proud of something you've put work into and made happen. It makes you a bit more interesting. Everybody else at a party might be mooching around talking about Netflix and you've been building an international business, that's really cool and really fun. It gives you travel opportunities, it gives you that real second wind when you start learning, networking and hanging out with a different crowd of people. A global bunch of entrepreneurial thinkers. It's really energizing to spend time with really sharp people who are looking to improve themselves and create products and services that are quality, and really smart businesses.

Make sure if you are going to start a business, you start something that's smart, something that's scalable and not just dependent on you. As well as making sure it's the right business model for your personality and skills, otherwise you'll find it a real slog and it won't be nearly so rewarding.

The Freedom Navigator course will take you through everything from really clarifying your profile, knowing your own strengths and being a bit more self aware, right through to all the different kinds of business models out there. How to get started with them, how to master all these different areas of online business. Not all of these business models are right for everyone and the trick is really picking the one that's right for you. That's where this course will help you get off to the right start, on the right tracs and building a business that's going to work for you.

You shouldn't work for your business, your business should work for you. And that's what we want from Freedom Navigator, to help you find your own track to financial freedom. We'll see you in the course, if you're ready to do this. Really looking forward to helping you and I hope you've learned some useful things in this book. I really enjoy sharing what I've learnt, through the ups and downs of the last few years as a business owner, mainly selling information products or physical products. I haven't done too much freelancing or consulting, but a little bit.

I've certainly found that focusing on the right business model and putting the most time and effort into the products and services, has been the best payoff. Whereas a lot of other smaller stuff that has a lot of noise around it, doesn't always make a big difference to the bottom line or what happens at the end of the day.

Make sure you focus on the stuff that matters, which business model, which industry, and get the best products and services that you're capable of producing. Then get out there and market them and make some big changes to your life by generating some additional income, making a business that you're really proud of. It can change your life. So, congratulations for finishing the book. It's been really fun sharing everything in here that I've learnt over the last few years and I hope you've learned something useful.

Printed in Great Britain
by Amazon